P9-CRA-365

TEACHING THE ESSENTIALS OF READING WITH PICTURE BOOKS

15 Lessons That Use Favorite Picture Books to Teach Phonemic Awareness, Phonics, Fluency, Comprehension, and Vocabulary

By Alyse Sweeney

New York • Toronto • London • Auckland • Sydney
Mexico City • New Delhi • Hong Kong • Buenos Aires

Teaching Resources

ACKNOWLEDGMENTS

Thank you, Peggy, Kerri, Jennifer, Diane, Jo, Randy, and Jamie,
for sharing your expertise and allowing the voices from your classrooms
to inspire and guide others in their classrooms.

Contents

Chapter 5: READING COMPREHENSION

Bibliography

Introduction

When you think of the classroom favorite *Stellaluna* by Janell Cannon, do you first think of using it to teach a lesson on how to use context clues? Do you immediately think of teaching a fluency lesson with Pat Hutchins' *The Wind Blew*? Probably not. And why should you? These books are not written for the purpose of teaching context clues, fluency skills, or any other reading skill, for that matter. Picture books are written to delight and awaken the imagination of young readers. They are written to inform and inspire. And that's why read-aloud time is such a cherished part of the school day for teachers and students.

But think about the additional treasures picture books reveal when you revisit them and read for a different purpose—to awaken children's understanding of how our language works. The same books you and your students love to read over and over may also be powerful vehicles for teaching comprehension strategies that help build proficiency and a love of reading. They can also be used to explore spelling patterns, analyze word endings, segment sounds, sharpen comprehension by understanding question-answer relationships, and so much more. According to Lucy Calkins, author of *The Art of Teaching Reading*, the read-aloud is the heart of reading instruction time.

The reading skills presented in this book are based on the five building blocks of reading outlined in the Reading First initiative, a component of the federally legislated No Child Left Behind Act (2000). The five building blocks are phonemic awareness, phonics, fluency, vocabulary, and text comprehension. *Put Reading First: The Research Building Blocks for Teaching Children to Read* is a U.S. Department of Education guide written by and for teachers that describes "what works" in reading instruction. (For a copy, visit <www.ed.gov> or call 877-433-7827.) The guide is a compilation of scientifically based research on the five areas of reading instruction. (See page 10 for more details about the five building blocks of reading.) The lessons in *Teaching the Essentials of Reading With Picture Books* incorporate best practices and explicit instruction that target the five areas of reading.

In *Teaching the Essentials of Reading With Picture Books*, talented teachers share how they teach reading skills with favorite picture books. Each lesson includes

- an explanation of the featured reading skill,

- step-by-step lesson instructions,

- lesson modifications that provide both a support and a challenge,

❏ recommended activities to further explore the reading skill,

❏ a short bibliography of picture books suitable for teaching the reading skill.

Many of the lessons are also accompanied by a reproducible page and dialogue from the lesson showing the lesson in action.

So take advantage of the fact that children love having you read to them. Continue to read aloud for sheer enjoyment. Then dive back into class favorites with a different purpose—to unlock the mysteries behind the five building blocks of reading. Which picture books in your library are waiting to play an even bigger role in helping your students succeed as readers?

Teaching Reading Through Reading Aloud

"The single most important activity for building the knowledge required for eventual success in reading is reading aloud to children." (*Becoming a Nation of Readers*, Anderson et al., 1985)

Here are guidelines for getting the best results from teaching reading through reading aloud.

1. **Assess what students need.** As with all instruction, determining the needs of your students is your first step. Students who read smoothly and with expression will gain little from the fluency lessons in this book. Other students, however, will benefit greatly from repeated exposure to the fluency lessons presented here. The list of recommended books that accompanies each lesson will make it easy for you to repeat the lessons using different picture books.

2. **Vary group size.** The lessons in this book can be taught to whole groups, small groups, and individuals. Many of the lessons are built around picture books that are also available in big-book format, allowing for whole-group instruction. Small-group instruction is particularly suitable when you want to teach the lesson to a group of students who share the same instructional needs, when you want to provide more opportunities for student participation, or when a big book is not available. Students will relish the attention of reading and exploring a favorite picture book in one-on-one instruction.

3. **Incorporate your regularly scheduled read-aloud time into the lessons.** For the most part, the reading lessons in this book occur during at least the second reading of the picture book. It is imperative that a student's first encounter with a read-aloud book be solely about enjoying the story or poem. The first reading of a book is devoted to focusing on the author's message and talking about favorite parts of the story, not segmenting onsets and rimes, looking for context clues, or analyzing spelling patterns. Therefore, depending on the length of the book and your time constraints, you may want to conduct the first reading during your regularly scheduled read-aloud time. The second reading of the book, accompanied by the reading lesson, can take place later that day or the following day.

4. **Set a purpose for reading.** Reading First requires teachers to be intentional and explicit when delivering reading instruction. Each lesson in this book is accompanied by a stated purpose for reading, such as "Listen to *Stellaluna* and practice using clues in the story to figure out unknown words." When you share with students the purpose of reading, they bring a focus to the lesson that helps them learn.

5. **Provide opportunities to practice the reading skills.** Each lesson is accompanied by activities to help students develop the featured reading skill. The activities are playful and some further involve picture books. Modify activities as needed to meet the needs of your students, or create your own activities that target particular skills.

6. **Allow students to interact with the book.** After children have a book read to them, they like to interact with the book up close. Display the book and allow students to read the book on their own.

7. **Make your own picture book/reading lesson match-ups!** Go beyond the picture books and reading skills presented here and make your favorite picture books the stars of explicit reading lessons. See page 9 for tips on choosing picture books to use in reading lessons.

Choosing Books for Reading Lessons

How do you select books to revisit for the purpose of teaching the five components of reading? Here are a few tips:

- ❏ Keep in mind that you always want to choose books that students will enjoy for their own sake. If your students love the characters, story, language, message, humor, or illustrations, they'll love to linger with the book and explore it on a different level. If the book does little to get their attention, the lesson will not have the same impact.

- ❏ Choose quality children's literature that is intended to be read aloud. This way, students can focus on both the author's intended meaning and on the book's rich or playful language.

- ❏ Look for a high concentration of the features you are looking for, such as many words beginning with the same letter or with the endings that you are teaching. In general, the more examples there are, the easier it is to pull together a lesson or activity, and the more opportunities there are for you to model the reading skill and for your students to practice it. However, even a book with few examples of the targeted reading element can be useful. The important thing is to draw the students' attention to the reading focus and to provide them with the opportunity to engage in words and written language in a direct and strategic way.

- ❏ Some books are suitable for exploring more than one reading element. Take Nancy Shaw's *Sheep on a Ship*: You can readily use the book to segment sounds in one lesson, locate words with the /sh/ letter combination in another lesson, and build fluency with echo reading in yet another lesson. Students will love any reason to revisit favorite books.

- ❏ Take into account the length of the book. A book that is too wordy may overwhelm students and make it difficult to locate and highlight the reading element you want to teach.

- ❏ More information on all books used in the lessons can be found in the Bibliography beginning on page 95.

The Five Building Blocks of Reading: An Overview

What does scientifically based research say about basic reading skills and instruction in the areas of phonemic awareness, phonics, fluency, vocabulary, and text comprehension? The overviews on the following pages are adapted from the findings in *Put Reading First: The Research Building Blocks for Teaching Children to Read.* (For a copy of the guide, visit <www.ed.gov> or call 877-433-7827.)

Phonemic Awareness	
What is phonemic awareness?	Phonemic awareness is an awareness of individual sounds in spoken language and the ability to manipulate those sounds.
Why is phonemic awareness instruction important?	If children are going to be successful readers, they must understand that words are made up of sounds, or phonemes. Some studies have shown that children who lack phonemic awareness in first grade are more likely to have reading difficulties in fourth grade. Further, phonemic awareness makes it easier for children to benefit from phonics instruction (a focus on the relationship between letters and their sounds).
How can I help students develop phonemic awareness?	Below are some activities to help students become aware of and manipulate sounds in spoken language: • **Identify phonemes:** *What sound is the same in* ball, boy, *and* bed? • **Blend phonemes to form words:** *What word is /s/ /u/ /n/?* (Have students write and read the word.) • **Segment words into phonemes:** *How many sounds are in* desk? *(Have students say each sound as they tap or count it. Then have them read and write the word.)* • **Add, delete, and substitute phonemes to make new words:** *What word do you have if you add /s/ to the beginning of* top? *What word is* plate *without the /p/? If you start with the word* pet *and change /t/ to /n/, what is the new word?*
What else do I need to know about phonemic awareness?	Below are ways to get the most out of phonemic awareness instruction: • Have students use letters as they manipulate phonemes to solidify the connection between phonemic awareness and reading and writing. • Teach one or two types of phoneme manipulation, not more, to avoid confusion. • Determine what students need in terms of instruction. One of the best ways to assess phonological awareness is by looking at children's writing. • Provide time for students to write. Writing requires them to segment phonemes and represent spoken sounds with letters. • Explore a variety of language features through reading aloud. Books with rhyme, repetition, alliteration, and sound-play are great choices.

University of Saint Francis-Ft. Wayne IN

Teaching the Essentials of Reading With Picture Books Scholastic Teaching Resources

Phonics

What is phonics?	Phonics is the relationship between speech sounds and their spellings.
Why is phonics instruction important?	Children who understand the relationship between letters and sounds are better able to read words accurately and figure out new words.
How can I help students develop phonics skills?	Phonics instruction is most effective when it is both systematic and explicit. • A *systematic* phonics program identifies a useful set of major letter-sound relationships in a clear sequence. The set of letter-sound relationships includes both consonants and vowels. • An *explicit* phonics program provides teachers with a plan for teaching children how to use their letter-sound knowledge to read and write words.
What else do I need to know about phonics instruction?	Children need many opportunities to read and write in order to apply their phonics skills. When selecting practice reading material, look for short books or stories that contain many examples of the letter-sound relationships children are learning. Phonics instruction can be given to individuals, small groups, or the whole class, depending on the needs of your students.

Fluency

What is fluency?	Fluency is the ability to read text quickly and accurately with comprehension and expression.
Why is fluency instruction important?	Decoding words effortlessly and using proper phrasing, pauses, and intonation all lead to better reading comprehension.
How can I help students develop fluency?	There are two main ways to help students become fluent readers: • Model fluent reading: As you read, talk about why you clump certain words together, change your voice, and pause. Then have children practice reading the text with the same expression, pauses, and intonation. • Guide oral reading: Students need many opportunities to practice reading short texts (50 to 200 words) that are written at their independent reading level (read with 95% accuracy). As students read aloud, they receive guidance and feedback from an adult or fluent reader.
What else do I need to know about fluency instruction?	Students need fluency instruction if they: 1) read without expression; 2) fail to recognize more than 10% of the words as they orally read an unfamiliar text; or 3) do not understand much of what they read orally. There are many motivating ways for students to practice oral reading, such as echo and choral reading, Reader's Theater, tape-recorded readings, and partner reading.

Vocabulary

What is vocabulary?	Vocabulary is a group of words we must know to communicate effectively.
Why is vocabulary instruction important?	If children do not know the meanings of the words they read, they will have trouble understanding what they read.
How can I help students build their vocabulary?	Children learn the meaning of words both indirectly and directly. **Indirect vocabulary learning:** students pick up the meaning of most words through exposure to everyday oral and written language. The more words they encounter in oral language and print, the more vocabulary they learn. You can promote indirect vocabulary learning when you • provide many opportunities for oral language. • read aloud to students often and talk about the books. • encourage students to read on their own. **Direct vocabulary learning:** Students also need to be taught difficult and unfamiliar words. Vocabulary can be taught directly through *specific word instruction* as well as *word-learning strategies.* Here are three keys to *specific word instruction:* • Teach vocabulary words *before* students encounter the words in a text for effective word learning and reading comprehension. • Give students many opportunities to use the new words actively over extended periods of time. • Teach the vocabulary words often, in a variety of contexts. Here are three ways to teach students *word-learning strategies*: • Teach students to use dictionaries and other resources. • Reinforce their knowledge of word parts. • Provide context clues.
What else do I need to know about vocabulary instruction?	It is more effective to directly teach just a few vocabulary words from a given text rather than all the words students do not know. Teach words from the following categories: 1) important words (words that are central to understanding the text); 2) useful words (words students will see over time); and 3) difficult words (words with multiple meanings, words with the same spelling or pronunciation but different meanings, and idiomatic expressions).

Teaching the Essentials of Reading With Picture Books Scholastic Teaching Resources

Text Comprehension

What is text comprehension?	Text comprehension (reading comprehension) is understanding the meaning of what is read. Reading is a pointless task without text comprehension.
Why is text comprehension instruction important?	Text comprehension instruction helps children become purposeful readers (reading for a variety of purposes) and active readers (using their experiences and knowledge of the world and of reading strategies to understand what they read).
How can I help students strengthen their text comprehension?	Teach students these six effective text comprehension strategies: • *Monitoring comprehension* helps them become aware of what they do understand, what they don't understand, and how to use strategies to fix comprehension problems. • *Graphic and semantic organizers* help them focus on concepts presented in the text, see the visual relationships in a text, and write organized text summaries. • *Answering questions* about what they read helps them read with purpose, think actively while they read, monitor their comprehension, and relate what they learned to prior knowledge. • *Generating questions* helps them think about their understanding of the text and whether or not they can answer the questions. • *Recognizing story structure* helps them appreciate, understand, and remember stories; categorize content by setting, initiating events, outcomes, and so on; and analyze the plot. • *Summarizing* helps them identify and generate main ideas, make connections between main ideas, differentiate between necessary and redundant or unnecessary information, and remember what they read.
What else do I need to know about text comprehension instruction?	Text comprehension instruction is most effective when it is explicit. Tell students why, when, what, and how strategies should be used. Students benefit when they are taught to adjust comprehension strategies when needed and use these strategies along with other strategies. Students can practice using comprehension strategies in cooperative learning groups.

Chapter 1

Phonemic Awareness

With an awareness of individual sounds in spoken language and the ability to manipulate those sounds, students are primed to be successful readers—and spellers. Fortunately, there are many fun and effective activities that can build phonemic awareness.

Since the goal of phonemic awareness instruction is to help students really notice sounds and masterfully manipulate them, playing with sounds is at the heart of phonemic awareness instruction. So have fun with the following phonemic awareness games and activities, and use them as jumping-off points for your own amusing versions.

Playing With Sounds to Build Phonemic Awareness

Teach Students to

Identify phonemes

Segment onsets and rimes

Manipulate phonemes

With Picture Books

Some Smug Slug by Pamela Duncan Edwards

Sheep on a Ship by Nancy Shaw

Jamberry by Bruce Degen

Teaching Phoneme Identity

With *Some Smug Slug* by Pamela Duncan Edwards

Presented by Jennifer Gibbons and her first-grade class

There are many fun ways to teach phoneme identity. Phonemes are the smallest part of sound in language, and phoneme identification is the ability to recognize the same sound in different words. When students attend to beginning sounds, they come to understand that sounds in words come in a particular order. They also become aware of the fact that changing the order of the sounds changes the word altogether.

Reading specialist Jennifer Gibbons chose *Some Smug Slug* to teach this phoneme identity lesson because it is an alliterative book.

Alliteration is a particularly powerful and engaging way to focus students' attention on beginning sounds. Alliteration occurs when two or more words in a series begin with the same sound. Some alliterative books highlight a variety of beginning sounds, while others, like this book, shine the spotlight on just one beginning sound. Jennifer also chose *Some Smug Slug* for its focus on the letter *s*, a difficult sound to master. She knew her students would love the playfulness of this book, and the sheer number of *s* words—103, to be exact!

LESSON

❑ Review with students the sound the letter *s* makes. Explain that the story they are about to listen to has many *s* words, or words that begin with the letter *s*. Exaggerate the beginning /s/ as you read the title *Some Smug Slug*. Tell the students that as you read the book you will provide them with a picture and a word that will remind them of the sound the letter *s* makes. On the top of a sheet of chart paper, draw and label a sun.

❑ Read *Some Smug Slug* aloud for fun.

❑ Before you reread the story, set the purpose: *to listen for words that begin with the /s/ sound.* Tell the class that this time as you read, they are going to count the *s* words on their fingers. Have the children hold their hands in the air in front of them and follow along with you as you model counting the eight *s* words on pages 4 and 5: "One summer Sunday while strolling on soil with its antennae signaling, a slug sensed a slope." For pages 4 and 5 only, have a volunteer hold the book so that your fingers are free for counting as you read the text. It is important to read each word slowly and pause briefly between words. Show the students how to compare any words they are not sure about to the word *sun* written at the top of the chart paper.

❑ After establishing that there are eight *s* words on pages 4 and 5, ask, "How many *s* words did you count? Can anyone tell me one of the *s* words you heard on these two pages?" Write the students' responses on large chart paper. Continue until there are no more volunteers. Ask, "Do we have eight words that start with the letter *s*? Let's count them." If there are not eight words, cross-check the list with the *s* words in the text until they are all listed. Repeat this process with the rest of the book.

On occasion, say two words from the text that begin with an *s* and one word that does not, such as *strolling, antennae, slope*. Can students tell you which words begin the same way and which word begins differently?

Lesson Modifications

Provide extra support: Have students who are really struggling listen to a recording of the book. Sometimes students focus better when they hear the story read by a different narrator or at a slower pace. Students can listen to the tape before the class lesson to build familiarity with the book or after the lesson for reinforcement.

Provide a challenge: Students who can readily discriminate the /s/ sound can then listen for *s* blends. On page 7, for example, there are three words beginning with *st*, and on page 15 there are three instances of *sl*.

Activities for Identifying Phonemes

1. Sort Those Words! Write a number of words from a story on index cards. On a pocket chart, display two headings: "Words That Begin With *S*" and "Words That Do Not Begin With *S*" (or whichever letter you are targeting). Have the students listen as you read the word on a card, then tell you where the word belongs in the chart. Have volunteers put the card under the correct heading.

2. Hear It, Write It. After reading a book that targets a particular letter sound, provide the children with copies of a picture that begins with the letter you are targeting, such as a drawing of the sun for *Some Smug Slug*. As you slowly read the story a second time, stop after each spread and have students write on the sun three *s* words that they heard. The number of words you ask them to write will vary with the book and level of the students. At the end, compare the students' lists, as they will all be different.

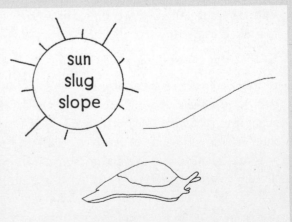

3. Write Tongue Twisters! After reading a slew of tongue twisters or a book like *Some Smug Slug*, have students try writing their own tongue twisters beginning with the letter you are targeting. Then have a tongue twister party at which students share their illustrated tongue twisters with the class!

More Books to Teach Beginning Sounds

A Pair of Protoceratops by Bernard Most (Harcourt Brace, 1998). In this delightful alliterative book, a pair of protoceratops practice penmanship, pester their papa, and plunge into pools. *A Trio of Triceratops* is the companion book.

Six Snowy Sheep by Judith Ross Enderle and Stephanie Gordon Tessler (Puffin Books, 1995). What happens when sheep sit on a sled, slip on skates, strap on skis, step into snowshoes, and settle into a saucer? They smoosh into a snowbank!

Busy Buzzing Bumblebees and Other Tongue Twisters by Alvin Schwartz (Harper & Row, 1982). Tangle your tongue with all 46 tongue twisters, such as "Six sharp smart sharks!"

Segmenting Onsets and Rimes

With *Sheep on a Ship* by Nancy Shaw

Presented by Kerri Moser and her first-grade class

To be successful readers, students need to recognize that words are made up of sounds. When words are segmented, or broken apart, the sounds are easier to hear. Words can be segmented into individual phonemes (/m/ /a/ /t/), syllables (*mat* has one syllable), and onsets and rimes (*m at*). The onset is the initial consonant sound of a syllable, and the rime is the part of a syllable that has the vowel and the letters that follow. When students identify and work with onsets and rimes in spoken words, they learn that words are made up of parts. Breaking up and putting together word parts makes it easier to read and write words.

Reading specialist Kerri Moser chose *Sheep on a Ship* for a lesson on segmenting onsets and rimes because this silly story about sheep that run into trouble at sea has little text per page, and is unique in that all pairs of rhyming words share the same spelling, making it easy to incorporate a word-family chart into this lesson. Kerri's lesson incorporates all the rhyming words in the book, but you can adjust your lesson according to the abilities of your students and time constraints.

LESSON

❑ Introduce *Sheep on a Ship* and conduct a picture walk.

❑ Read the story aloud for sheer enjoyment.

❑ Before you reread the story, conduct a mini-lesson on breaking words apart. On the chalkboard or at the top of chart paper, write the word *cat* with the onset (*c*) in one color and the rime (*at*) in a different color. Explain that the word *cat* has two parts, *c* and *at*. Articulate the segmenting as you read the word and point out the parts. Have the class say the sounds of the two word-parts along with you. Now demonstrate how to use sound to represent each word-part by clapping for the onset and slapping your thighs for the rime. Invite the students to clap and slap the word *cat* several times. Repeat these steps for a few more words.

❑ Now set the purpose for the reading: *to listen for rhyming words, decide where the words go on the chart, and clap and slap the word parts*. Explain that students should listen for rhyming words and help you decide which word family they belong in (see the chart on page 22). After all the rhyming words are recorded on the chart, the class will clap and slap the word parts together.

- Make a transparency or reproducible of the word family chart on page 22, or make your own large version. Explain that all the rhyming words in this book have an ending word-part that matches one of the eight word families (-ip, -ap, -orm, -ails, -ide, -aft, -ifts, and -o).

- Read the first page of the book, which begins on page 7: "Sheep sail a ship on a deep-sea trip." Guide students to find the rhymes. Explain that they're listening for two words that sound alike. Read the sentence slowly, clearly articulating each word and placing emphasis on the words *ship* and *trip*. After *ship* and *trip* have been identified as rhyming words, ask students where to write *ship* and *trip* on the chart. If they need assistance, slowly say *ship* and *trip* and then name the first word family on the chart (-ip). Have students tell you if the words rhyme with -ip, or if you should try the next word family. Continue as needed, and write the words under the appropriate word family using two colors.

- Continue rounding up the rhymes and recording them on the chart for each page.

- Now slowly clap and slap the -ip words. Clap and slap them again a little faster. Continue with each group of words. Invite volunteers to clap and slap groups of words. Can children think of other ways to break the words with sound, such as finger-snapping and foot-tapping?

Segmenting Onsets and Rimes
With *Sheep on a Ship* by Nancy Shaw

-ip	-ap	-orm	-ails
ship	lap	form	hails
trip	flap	storm	sails
slip	map		rails
tip	nap		
whip			
rip			
drip			

-ide	-aft	-ifts	-o
glide	raft	lifts	land-ho
collide	craft	drifts	go

LESSON IN ACTION

After reading the story the first time:

Miss Moser: Now I want to explain something to you. There were words in this story that we can have a lot of fun with. We can take these words and break them apart. I want you to take a look at this board with these magnetic letters and see what this word is here. If you know the word, please read it.

Class: *Cat*.

Miss Moser: *Cat*. Well, this word cat can be broken up into parts. Breaking words into parts can help us to read words. I think we can break this word up easily. Chrystal, would you like to try?

Chrystal: If you take away the *c* and leave that /a/ /t/, it would be *at*.

Miss Moser: That's right. If you take away the *c* and leave the /a/ /t/, it would be *at*. So you found a part of the word. Which

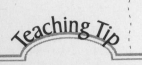

part of the word did she find, the first part or the last part? Leanne?

Leanne: The last part.

Miss Moser: Good job. She found the last part. Let's take a look at the first part. Let's break that word up into /c/ /at/. The first part is /c/ (_claps as she says sound_). Okay, we have /c/ for the first part, and here we clap. The second part is /at/, so we slap. Now watch Miss Moser—/C/ (clap) /at/ (slap). <u>Cat</u>. Now you try it.

Class: /C/ (clap) /at/ (slap). <u>Cat</u>.

Miss Moser: You didn't sound so certain. Try again.

Class: /C/ (clap) /at/ (slap). <u>Cat</u>.

Miss Moser: Sounds good!

Lesson Modifications

Provide extra support: Simplify the lesson by focusing on fewer word families. Students who have difficulty segmenting onsets and rimes can practice physically making and breaking words with magnetic or other manipulable letters. Model how to construct and break the word. Then articulate each part separately. Finally, articulate the word as a whole. Students can work in pairs, in small groups, or independently.

Provide a challenge: Have a small group of students clap and slap to the text itself, not to the chart. After reading a page and locating the rhymes, point to the first rhyming word as you say it. When you say the word a second time, the students clap and slap the word. Continue for the other rhyming words.

More Activities for Segmenting Onsets and Rimes

1. People Letters. In this activity, students wear paper onsets and rimes and come together to make words. On large, sturdy paper, write the onset and rimes of a variety of words from a rhyming book you have read and explored with the class. Punch two holes at the top and tie a loop of string to create a hanging letter costume. At the front of the room, have the beginning word parts stand to the right and ending word parts stand to the left. Say a word, such as _ship_, from a rhyming book you have recently read and guide the correct onset (_sh_) and rime (_ip_) to come together to make the word. Have both students say in unison the word they made. To make the next word, change the onset of the previous word. When one word family has been exhausted, move to another word family.

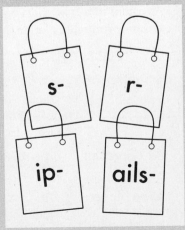

Teaching the Essentials of Reading With Picture Books Scholastic Teaching Resources

2. Teams of Onsets and Rimes. On large cards, write several words from the same word family. Use one color for the onset and another color for the rime (for example, red and blue). Divide the class into two teams and assign one team to say the red part of the word and the other team to say the blue part of the word. Then have the entire class say the word together. Have students vary the way they say the words. For example, each side may whisper the onset and rime and then shout the word. Also vary the way you divide the class in teams of onsets and rimes (students on the left and students on the right, students in the front and students in the back, students whose shoes have laces and students wearing any other kind of shoe, and so on).

3. Breaking Words With Magnetic Letters. Provide the class with magnetic letters to make several words from one or two word families. Model how to make the words and break them into their beginning and ending parts. Articulate each part separately, and finally articulate the entire word. Allow students to work in pairs or small groups. Be sure to give the class specific, direct instruction during modeling. Let students have the chance to practice with you present before you leave them to work independently.

More Books for Teaching Segmenting Onsets and Rimes

A Huge Hog Is a Big Pig: A Rhyming Word Game by Francis McCall and Patricia Keeler (Greenwillow Books, 2002). As soon as you open this book, word game fun begins: "A wet hound is a . . . soggy doggy. A silly rabbit is a . . . funny bunny."

Big Bear Ball by Joanne Ryder (HarperCollins Publishers, 2002). There are lots of opportunities to explore word families in this rollicking text about a bear bash: "Now thump those stumps and wake those moles. Let's rouse the foxes from their holes."

Green Eggs and Ham by Dr. Seuss (Random House, 1960). "I do not like them in a box. I do not like them with a fox." Kids love playing with beginning and ending sounds in this Seuss classic.

Segmenting Onsets and Rimes

With *Sheep on a Ship* by Nancy Shaw

-ip	-ap	-orm	-ails

-ide	-aft	-ifts	-o

Teaching the Essentials of Reading With Picture Books Scholastic Teaching Resources

Teaching Phoneme Manipulation

With *Jamberry* by Bruce Degen

Presented by Diane Marzigliano and her second-grade class

There are five progressively more difficult levels of phonemic awareness tasks, and phonemic manipulation tasks are the most complex. They require students to add, delete, or substitute phonemes to create another word. These tasks provide strong predictions of beginning reading acquisition (Adams, 1994).

Jamberry is a jamboree of rhyming words.

With sentences such as *"Quickberry! Quackberry! Pick me a blackberry,"* Diane Marzigliano can't resist using this book to explore phoneme manipulation in the beginning and middle of words. Her students adore this story about a boy and a bear on a berry-picking mission and delight in playing with these delicious words.

LESSON

Preparation

❑ In the book itself, place highlighting tape over the words on which this lesson will focus: *dam, jam* (page 5), *Quickberry, Quackberry* (page 14), *Trainberry, Trackberry* (page 15), *Rumble, ramble, bramble, jamble* (page 18), *berryband, merryband* (page 19), *boomberry, zoomberry* (page 24), and *Mountains, fountains* (page 25).

❑ Write each of the words on a card, but exclude the beginning or middle phonemes that are to be manipulated. These word cards will be used in a pocket chart: _____am, Qu_____ckberry, Tr____berry, r____mble, ____amble, _____erryband, _____oomberry, _____ountains.

❑ Create a card for each of the following letters or letter groups: *d, j, i, a, ain, ack, u, b, j, m, z, f.*

Phoneme Manipulation Mini-Lesson

Write the word *jam* on the board. Ask students whether it looks or sounds like another word they know (*ham, dam, yam, Pam, Sam, clam*). Choose one answer and ask a volunteer to write the new word (e.g., *ham*) under the word *jam*. Ask the student how the word is similar to *jam* and how it is different. Ask how the child changed the word *jam* to create the word *ham*. Have another volunteer change the middle sound in *ham* to create a new word and write the word on the board, e.g. *him*. Elicit from the students how they created the new words. How are *ham* and *him* the same and different? Lead students to realize that changing beginning and middle phonemes creates new words. Have them tell you what they have just learned.

◻ Read the story aloud for enjoyment. Students will likely question why some words are highlighted. Explain that they will find out when you read them the story the second time.

◻ Before revisiting the book, set the purpose: *to learn how words change when beginning and middle letters change.* Tell the students they will now try to discover why some of the rhyming words in the story have been highlighted.

◻ Read to the end of page 5, where *dam* and *jam* are highlighted. Ask the students what they notice about these two words. How are they the same? How are they different? Someone should notice that one word begins with a *d* and the other begins with a *j*. Ask the students to identify the part of the word where these letter differences are found. Place the *am* word card on the chart. Have a student come to the board and select and manipulate the letter needed to spell the word *dam*. Have another volunteer select the letter needed to change the word *dam* to *jam*. Explain that changing and replacing letters in words makes new words, and therefore new meanings. Ask, *Do the words dam and jam mean the same thing?*

◻ Continue through the story in the same manner, posing similar questions when encountering the highlighted words and inviting students to the pocket chart to demonstrate how manipulating phonemes in words can make new words. Conclude the lesson with questions such as these: *What have you learned? How can we make a new word? What part of a word can we change to make a new word? Do we have to change all parts of a word to create a new word?*

LESSON IN ACTION

After reading page 14: "Quickberry! Quackberry! Pick me a blackberry!"

Ms. Marzigliano: These two words have special tape on them. Christopher, do you know why these words have special tape on them?

Christopher: They both look the same, but they're not.

Ms. Marzigliano: Okay. How do they both look the same? Can you explain that?

Christopher: Because *quick* and *quack* only look the same, but they're not.

Ms. Marzigliano: Excellent. How are they different?

Christopher: Because *quick* has /i/ /c/ /k/ and *quack* has /a/ /c/ /k/.

Ms. Marzigliano: Excellent, Christopher! Can you come up and make the word *quickberry*?

Christopher: This one? (_picking up the_ Qu_____ckberry _word card_)

Ms. Marzigliano: Yes. What do you think we need to make the word _quickberry_? Look at it carefully. You said that _quickberry_ has the /ick/. But what is helping it to have the /ick/, and what is helping _quackberry_ to have the /ack/? What is actually different? Do you notice what is different?

Christopher: The /c/ /k/ is different.

Ms. Marzigliano: Well, do they both have /c/ /k/?

Christopher: Yes.

Ms. Marzigliano: So what is actually different?

Christopher: The /a/ and the /i/.

Ms. Marzigliano: The /a/ and the /i/. Are they in the beginning, middle, or end of the word?

Christopher: Middle.

Ms. Marzigliano: Can you please create the new word? Find the letter that's missing. Very good. Who would like to come up and change _quickberry_ to _quackberry_? Angelee? What letter are you going to change?

Angelee: I'm going to change the _i_ and I'm going to put the _a_ in the middle.

Ms. Marzigliano: Come over here and let me see how you are going to do that. Very good, Angelee. Read your new word.

Lesson Modifications

Provide extra support. Highlight only rhymed words in which the beginning letters are different. Once children have a handle on phoneme manipulation with initial letters, use words in the book that show changes in middle phonemes.

Provide a challenge. As students become familiar with word cards and with words from the book, ask them to think of other words that would fit into the same pattern, such as _truckberry_ in place of _trainberry_ and _trackberry_.

More Phoneme Manipulation Activities

1. Making Words: This is among the most effective phoneme manipulation activities. Give students letters for a six- to eight-letter word and have them follow your directions to add, delete, or substitute letters—change the _n_ in _in_ to make, for example, _is_. Begin with two-letter words and increase to three-, four-, and five-letter words. The final word includes all the letters of the six- to eight-letter word you chose.

From _Making Words_ by Patricia M. Cunningham and D.P. Hall.

2. Sound Sketch: Direct students to make words out of sounds and have them make a sketch for the words. For example:

❏ Add /t/ to the end of *an*. Sketch the word.

❏ Replace the /a/ in *map* with /o/. Sketch the word.

From *Rhymes & Reasons: Literature and Language Play for Phonological Awareness* by Michael F. Opitz

3. The Ever-Changing Word: At the top of chart paper, write a simple sentence, such as *Swimming is a <u>blast</u>* (underlining the last word in your sentence). Create a narrow column on the right side of the page. Ask a volunteer to change one or more consecutive letters in the word. Write the new word in the narrow column on the chart and ask the student to describe how it was formed. What letter (or letters) was added, taken away, or substituted? Now have the student use that word in a new sentence. Write the new sentence and underline the new word (*If you break a leg, you wear a <u>cast</u>.*) Have another volunteer change one or more letters of the underlined word, and repeat the steps. Talk about the different ways the word is changing, and encourage initial, medial, and final substitutions, deletions, and additions.

More Books to Teach Phoneme Manipulation

In the Small, Small Pond by Denise Fleming (H. Holt, 1993). This book about a busy pond offers fabulous examples of phoneme manipulation in the beginning and medial positions: "Sweep, swoop, swallows scoop. Click, clack, claws crack."

An Edward Lear Alphabet by Edward Lear (Lothrop, Lee & Shepard Books, 1983). This alphabet book playfully demonstrates phoneme substitution to the max: "A was once an apple pie, /Pidy/Widy/Tidy/Pidy/Nice insidy/Apple pie."

Up in the Air by Myra Cohn Livingston (Holiday House, 1989). Higher and higher the plane soars, revealing glorious views from an airplane seat. The three lines on every page end with a word from the same word family: "Off to the blue of the highest sky, /A thin curl of clouds passes us by. /Ruffled clouds chasing us, up we fly." Big Book.

Chapter 2

Phonics

Children who understand the predictable relationship between letters and sounds are better able to read words accurately and figure out new words. Engaging picture books are a great place to round up words and analyze their letters and corresponding sounds.

As with the previous phonemic awareness activities, the activities presented in this chapter are both explicit and playful. The picture books are carefully chosen to provide students with ample opportunities to practice the letter-sound relationships you present.

Playing With Sounds and Letters to Teach Phonics

Teach Students to

Identify sounds of letters

Focus on the letter combination *sh*

Analyze spelling patterns

With Picture Books

A Is for Salad by Mike Lester

Sheep on a Ship by Nancy Shaw

Nuts to You! by Lois Ehlert

Teaching the Sounds of Letters

With *A Is for Salad* by Mike Lester

Presented by Jamie Levine and her first-grade class

Alphabet recognition, or knowing the names of the letters and the sounds they stand for, is one of two powerful predictors of early reading success. The other predictor is phonemic awareness (Adams, 1994). In Chapter I, we explored how to use picture books to help students develop phonemic awareness and recognize that words are made up of sounds. In this lesson, the focus is on using picture books to teach the sound that is attached most frequently to each letter.

Alphabet books are a fun and effective tool with which beginning readers can learn letter names, letter forms, and letter-sound relationships. Today's alphabet books cover a wide range of topics, and some are written with an unconventional twist, such as *A Is for Salad*. *A* is for salad? Actually, *A* is for the alligator eating the salad. Unlike traditional alphabet books, this book keeps students on their toes and invites them to seek out the object in the picture that goes with the featured letter. The result is that students get double the practice with letter sounds as they discuss and reject the word that does not begin with the featured letter, and find the word that *really* begins with the featured letter. There are also lots of giggles along the way! In this lesson, Jamie Levine's first-graders use *A Is for Salad* as a model for their own class alphabet book.

LESSON

- ❑ Begin with a discussion about alphabet books. Ask students what all alphabet books have in common. What might be different? How are alphabet books different from story books? Can students recall the title of any alphabet books they have read before?

- ❑ Before reading the book, set the purpose for reading: *to find the object in the picture that begins with the featured letter.*

- ❑ Tell the children that this alphabet book is peculiar. Encourage them to listen carefully to learn why. Read the title of the book and three or four pages before eliciting ideas about what is different about the format of this alphabet book.

- ❑ After establishing the book's pattern—the letters do not stand for the word in the sentence, but rather for the animal in the picture—discuss why the author might have chosen this zany format. Responses may include: *to make the book more interesting, to be funny, to help the reader think about letters more,* or *to be different from other authors.* As you continue reading the book, draw the students' attention to the letter-sound relationships on each page.

❑ When you have finished reading the book, ask the students to raise their hands if they liked the way Mike Lester wrote this alphabet book. If your class is like Jamie's, they will be very enthusiastic about the book. Tell them that since they liked the book so much, they are going to create a class version of *A Is for Salad.*

Make a Class Alphabet Book

❑ Before you reread *A Is for Salad,* hand out a letter to each student, with the exception of *X* and *Y,* if you want to follow Mike Lester's lead. Extra letters can be handed out as rewards over the coming days. Reread the book, stopping after each page to guide students with the corresponding letter to think of another animal that begins with the same letter. If they need assistance, they can call on a classmate. Or you can give the students clues to help them think of an animal. On chart paper, keep track of the animals each student picks.

❑ Ask students to think about how their animal will interact with an object. Encourage them to make the relationship between the object and the animal in their picture silly, like the examples in the book. If they forget the animal they selected, they can look on the chart. Over the next several days, spend a few minutes talking to individual students about their ideas. Have *A Is for Salad* on hand so they can check the pattern of their page against the original book. Once you have approved the students' pages, have them write the text in the class book, as in *A is for* [the object the child selected], and then illustrate the page. Remind students to keep their pictures simple. Explain that a lot of detail or additional objects and animals may confuse the reader. Have them hold their pages horizontally, if you want the book to look like *A Is for Salad.*

❑ When all the pages are complete, assemble the book using staples, string, or clamps. Share the book with the class, with students reading their pages. Have the class share the book with other classes as well. The other students will delight in figuring out what each letter really stands for. Then display the book in the book corner for rereading.

LESSON IN ACTION...

Mrs. Levine: Today we are going to read an alphabet book. Who can tell me what an alphabet book is?

Trish: It's a book about the alphabet.

Mrs. Levine: Yes. An alphabet book is a book about the alphabet. And can anyone tell me what makes an alphabet book different from a storybook?

Sam: An alphabet book tells the sound of each letter. Like <u>A</u> is for <u>apple</u> and <u>B</u> is for <u>balloon</u>.

Mrs. Levine: That's right! Many alphabet books follow that pattern. Each letter is paired with a word that begins with the sound of that letter.

Amy: And each letter gets its own page.

Mrs. Levine: Exactly. The alphabet book we are going to read today is a little bit peculiar, or strange. Listen as I read a few pages and maybe you'll see what I mean. (<u>Mrs. Levine reads the title and up to the third page.</u>)

Mrs. Levine: Does anybody notice anything unusual about this alphabet book?

John: <u>Hot dog</u> does not begin with a <u>c</u>!

Mrs. Levine: No, it doesn't. What letter does <u>hot dog</u> begin with? Trevor?

Trevor: <u>H</u>.

Mrs. Levine: Let's go back to the <u>A</u> page. <u>A is for salad</u>. What is unusual here?

Jennifer: The letter doesn't match the word.

Mrs. Levine: Interesting.

Juan: Look! An alligator is eating the salad. Maybe he wants us to look closely at the pictures.

Mrs. Levine: Aha! An alligator is eating the salad.

Juan: And <u>alligator</u> starts with an <u>a</u>!

Mrs. Levine: So it seems we have to look closely at the pictures to find the word that begins with the featured letter, right? A isn't for salad, but it is for the alligator that is eating the salad. Why do you think the author, Mike Lester, wrote <u>A Is for Salad</u>?

Christina: Maybe to be different?

Mrs. Levine: Okay. Ben?

Ben: To be funny.

Mrs. Levine: Yes, this book is pretty silly, isn't it? Anyone else? Rachel?

Rachel: I think he wants us to search the pictures for clues.

Mrs. Levine: Good. He is not just going to tell us the word that each letter stands for. He wants us to find the picture of the thing that each letter stands for. Okay. So now we know that this is not like other alphabet books. We have to look very closely at the pictures to learn what each letter stands for, right? Let's all read together. Then we'll go around the circle and each of you will have a chance to say what each letter really stands for. Here we go.

Teaching the Essentials of Reading With Picture Books Scholastic Teaching Resources

Lesson Modifications

Provide extra support: If students are having a difficult time thinking of how their animal will interact with an object, have them revisit *A Is for Salad* for ideas. If they need more practice spacing words in a sentence, have them write their sentence on a sentence strip, cut up the words, put the words back into a sentence, and glue their sentence along the top of the page they are going to illustrate.

Provide a challenge: More advanced students can write their own alphabet book following Mike Lester's format, the format of another alphabet book, or their own format.

More Phonics Activities

1. **Fun with Alphabet Books.** There are many engaging alphabet books on the market today. Share a bunch with your students and have them decide which are their favorites and why. Create a class graph depicting favorites, or have students write book reviews.

2. **Have Children "Be" the Alphabet.** This is a great lining-up activity that helps students pair the written letters with the spoken letters. When the class needs to line up to go somewhere, hand each student a laminated letter card. (You keep the extra cards.) As the class slowly sings the alphabet song, the students line up when they hear their letter.

   From *Making Words* by Patricia M. Cunningham and D.P. Hall.

3. **Letter Hunt.** As you take the class on a walk around your school or neighborhood, have students identify letters in print they see around them.

More Alphabet Books with a Twist

It Begins with an A by Stephanie Calmenson (Hyperion Books for Children, 1993). Written as a riddle, this book is sure to invite enthusiastic class participation. "You travel in this. It begins with an A. It starts on the ground, then flies up, up away!"

Alphathoughts: Alphabet Poems by Lee Bennett Hopkins (Wordsong/Boyds Mills Press, 2003). Each playful one-line poem provides a definition of a word: "Reunion. A coming together to remember memories." Can your students find the additional word or words beginning with the same letter?

Aster Aardvark's Alphabet Adventure by Steven Kellogg (William Morrow, 1987). This alliterative adventure features a mini-story on each page: "Hermione, a hefty hippo, hurt her hip hurling herself into the Hawaiian Hula Hoop Happening." Great vocabulary.

Teaching Letter Combinations

With *Sheep on a Ship* by Nancy Shaw

Presented by Jo Kelchner and her first-grade class

Children's literature provides enjoyable opportunities to expose students to the predictable relationship between written letter combinations and the sounds they make. With explicit instruction, students come to learn that some letter combinations, such as *ph*, are highly reliable, almost always representing one sound, while others, such as *th*, represent two pronunciations. Some letter combinations, such as the blend *bl*, are a straightforward combination of two letters, while other letter combinations, such as the digraph *sh*, are two consonants that stand for a completely new sound when they appear together. When children learn that there is a systematic and predictable relationship between written letters and spoken sounds, they are better able to read words accurately and use letter-combination knowledge to read new words. Visual memory is also improved by explicit letter-combination instruction, resulting in better spelling.

Jo Kelchner uses *Sheep on a Ship* with her reading groups because of its playful and abundant use of *sh* words. In this lesson, her students use a shark prop to indicate when they hear a word with /sh/, and then sort word cards that begin and end in *sh*. Jo finds *Sheep on a Ship* an extremely motivating tool for helping students learn the *sh* digraph, an often confusing letter combination.

Preparation

1. Make copies of the Shark and Dish reproducibles on page 36. Place the pictures on a chart and attach a pocket for collecting word cards beneath each picture.

2. You'll also need one copy of the Shark alone from the reproducible on page 36. Glue or tape the shark to a craft stick. (I laminate mine so that I have them year after year.)

3. Create about five word cards that begin with *sh*, such as *shell, short, sheep, ship, shapes,* and five word cards that end with *sh*, such as *wash, flash, trash, fish, slosh.*

LESSON

❑ Read the story aloud for enjoyment.

❑ Before the second reading, set the purpose for reading: *to identify words that begin or end with* sh. Tell students that they are going to

Teaching the Essentials of Reading With Picture Books Scholastic Teaching Resources

listen for the words that begin and end in /sh/. Demonstrate the /sh/ sound and have each student repeat it.

❑ Give each child a shark prop. Instruct the class to hold up the shark when they hear a word that begins or ends with /sh/. As you reread the story, pause slightly at the words containing the /sh/ sound and stress it. Acknowledge the responses that the students make.

❑ When you reach the end of the book, ask the class to recall words from the book that have /sh/. As soon as words that both begin and end in /sh/ are suggested, ask students what they notice about the placement of /sh/ in each example. Continue adding to the list until most of the *sh* words from the book are mentioned.

❑ Now have students actively work with both kinds of *sh* words. One at a time, hold up your *sh* word cards as you slowly read the word. Select students to place the card in the pocket under the shark, if the word begins with *sh,* or under the dish, if the word ends with *sh.* Remind students to look and listen before sorting the word.

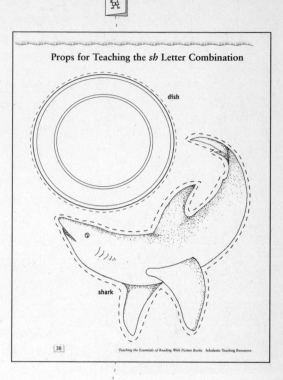

Props for Teaching the *sh* Letter Combination

dish

shark

36

Teaching the Essentials of Reading With Picture Books Scholastic Teaching Resources

LESSON IN ACTION

Mrs. Kelchner: I want to share a story with you today called <u>Sheep on a Ship</u>. I'm going to read this story to you and I want you to listen very carefully to a special sound—the sound made by the letters <u>s</u> and <u>h</u> together (<u>writing sh on the board</u>). Can anyone tell me what that sounds like? Anne Katherine?

Anne Katherine: <u>Shhhh</u>.

Mrs. Kelchner: Shhh. Everyone say that. Go like this with your finger over your mouth. Shhhhh. It is the sound you hear when someone wants you to be quiet. Shhh.

Class: Shhhhh.

Mrs. Kelchner: Very good. There are some words in this story, <u>Sheep on a Ship</u>, that have that sound in them. Listen carefully with your ears. Look carefully with your eyes. See if you can hear or see any words that have /sh/. I'm going to give you each a shark. And if you hear the sound of /sh/, either in the beginning or at the end of a word, I want you to hold up your shark. Okay, everyone show me what you are going to do if you hear a word that has the /sh/ sound. Show me what you are going to do. Very good! Hold it up nice and high!

After reading the book:

Mrs. Kelchner: Did you hear some /sh/ words in that story?

Class: Yes! A lot.

Mrs. Kelchner: Can you think of any /sh/ words in that story? Do you remember any of them? Delaney?

Delaney: _Ship_.

Mrs. Kelchner: _Ship_. Mike, can you tell me another one?

Mike: _Sheep_.

Mrs. Kelchner: _Sheep_. Tell me another one. Andrew?

Andrew: _Slip_.

Mrs. Kelchner: Is that a /sh/, sssslip? Is that /sh/?

Andrew: _Shake_.

Mrs. Kelchner: _Shake_. Great. Can you remember any other words from the story? Ian?

Ian: _Slosh._

Mrs. Kelchner: _Slosh_! Very good. What's the difference between these three words: _sheep_, _ship_, _shake_, and the word _slosh_? Ian?

Ian: They all have /sh/ in them?

Mrs. Kelchner: They all have /sh/ in them, but what's the difference between _shake_ and _slosh_? Delaney?

Delaney: _Slosh_ has /sh/ at the end.

Mrs. Kelchner: _Slosh_ has the /sh/ at the end. Where does _shake_ have the /sh/?

Delaney: At the beginning.

Mrs. Kelchner: At the beginning. Good listening.

Lesson Modifications

Provide extra support: When reading the story to younger readers, highlight the _sh_ words with highlighting tape and verbally stress the /sh/ sound.

Provide a challenge: Following the same lesson structure, have the students listen for and then classify the words that begin with /sh/ and the words that begin with /s/.

Word Games With Letter Combinations

1. **Word Sorts.** To vary the word-sort activity presented in this lesson, compare a letter combination with another potentially confusing letter or combination, such as words beginning with _sh_ and _s, ch_ and _c_, or _sh_ and _ch_. You can also sort letter combinations by the way they sound in different words, such as the /th/ in _their_ versus the /th/ in _Thursday_.

Teaching the Essentials of Reading With Picture Books Scholastic Teaching Resources

2. Letter-Combination Bingo. Provide each student with a blank nine-square Bingo game card. On the board, record a lengthy student-generated list of words with the targeted letter combinations, such as words with specific blends or digraphs. Students select words on this list to randomly write in the BINGO squares. As you call out a word, students place a chip in the appropriate square. When the student has three squares covered in a row, he or she calls out Bingo!

B	I N G	O
sheep	slosh	slip
sail	ship	sea
slide	shake	shore

3. Word Toss. This activity is great for reviewing several letter combinations. Tape five to ten paper cups to the floor so that they are touching. On the inside lip of each cup, in thick marker, write a letter combination, such as *bl*, *tw*, *qu*, or *ch*. Working in pairs or groups of three, students take turns tossing a button, coin, or chip into the cup and saying a word that begins or ends with that particular letter combination. They can individually record the words on letter-combination charts.

More Books for Teaching Letter Combinations

Mrs. McNosh Hangs up Her Wash by Sara Weeks (Laura Geringer Book, 1988). Every Monday morning, Mrs. McNosh hangs up her wash, along with two sleepy bats, grandpa's removable teeth, and much, much more. Revisit the text to find three words beginning with *sh* (*she*, *shirt*, and *shoes*) and three words ending in *sh* (*McNosh*, *wash*, and *dish*). Big Book.

The Very Clumsy Click Beetle by Eric Carle (Philomel Books, 1999). Little click beetle tries and tries to flip in the air and land on its feet. Finally, after a flip through the air and three graceful somersaults, it succeeds! After enjoying the story, find the words ending in *ck*: *click*, *back*, *stuck*, *luck*, and *quick*.

Raccoon Tune by Nancy Shaw (Henry Holt and Company, 2003). This story about a mischievous family of raccoons who prowl around the neighborhood looking for dinner is written in lively verse and filled with words with the silent *gh* letter combination (*moonlight*, *night*, *fright*, and *ought*, to name just a few).

Props for Teaching the *sh* Letter Combination

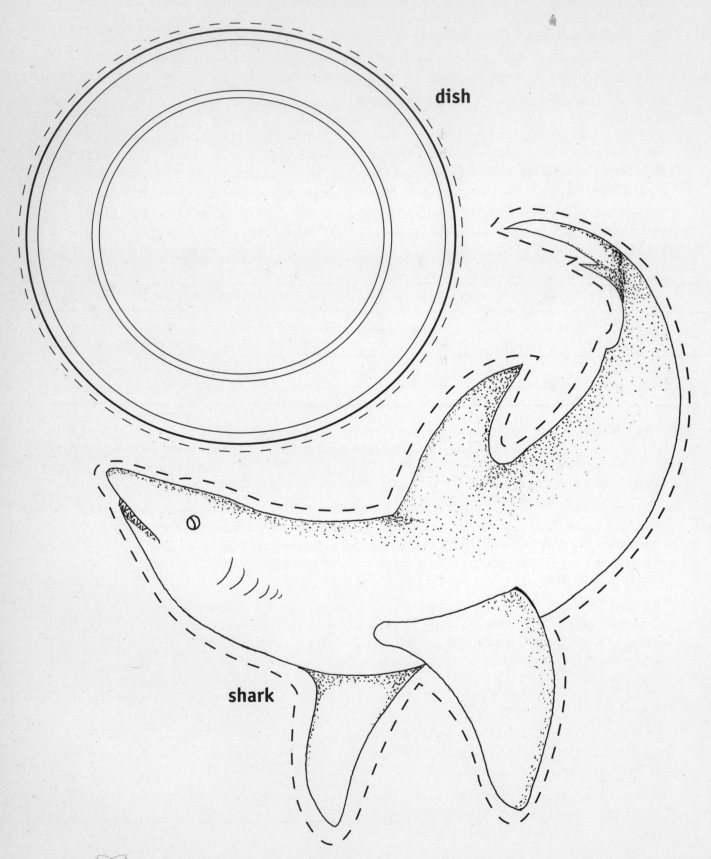

dish

shark

Analyzing Spelling Patterns

With *Nuts to You!* by Lois Ehlert

Presented by Kerri Moser and her first-grade class

P honics instruction helps students make sense of words that sound the same but are spelled differently (*high*, *cry*, *tie*, and *bye*). When children learn that there is a systematic and predictable relationship between written letters and spoken words, they are better able to read words accurately and use their knowledge of spelling patterns to read new words. Further, lessons that focus on spelling patterns help them sharpen their visual memory, a requirement for good spelling.

There are many reasons why reading specialist Kerri Moser chose *Nuts to You!* for a lesson on analyzing the spelling patterns of rhyming words. The story is engaging, there is a good balance of same and differently spelled rhyming words, the text is a manageable length, the type is large, and Lois Ehlert is one of her favorite authors. *Nuts to You!*, a story about a squirrel who pokes around an apartment, was inspired by an actual experience Lois Ehlert had with a squirrel in her neighborhood. The story has lots of energy and great rhythm. Kerri uses a graphic organizer to help students sort and analyze the rhyming words.

LESSON

❏ Read *Nuts to You!* aloud for pleasure.

❏ After establishing the fact that *Nuts to You!* is a rhyming book, ask the students if they think words that sound the same also need to be spelled the same. Can they provide examples to support their answer? After discussing their examples or providing your own, if needed, explain that *Nuts to You!* has lots of examples of both rhyming words that are spelled the same and rhyming words that are spelled differently.

❏ Before rereading the story, set the purpose for reading: *to find the rhyming words and decide if they have the same or a different spelling pattern.*

❏ Make a transparency or enlargement of the chart on page 40.

❏ As a class, read the first page slowly: "See that squirrel in our tree? I think he'd rather live with me." Articulate *tree* and *me* carefully.

❏ Ask a volunteer to approach the book and point to the rhyming words. In the Rhyming Words column on the chart, write *me* and

Rhyming Words and How They Are Spelled

Rhyming Words		Same Word Family	Different Word Families
cat	mat	✔ Word Family ___at	☐ Word Families ___ and ___
bear	lair	☐ Word Family _____	✔ Word Families _ear_ and _air_
_____	_____	☐ Word Family _____	☐ Word Families ___ and ___

tree. Now ask the volunteer if these rhyming words share the same word family. This rhyming pair is a little tricky, requiring students to look extra carefully to notice that *-ee* and *-e* are not the same. After it is established that *tree* and *me* do not share the same word family, put a check in the Different Word Family box and ask the student to tell you what the two word families are. Write *-ee* and *-e* on the lines.

◻ Repeat this process with the rest of the book.

LESSON IN ACTION

Miss Moser: I am going to read the book for the first time and you are going to listen. Then the second time you are going to help me by doing some searching. Your focus will be to find rhyming words and decide if they have the same or different spelling patterns. Sometimes two words rhyme, and even though they sound alike, they may not be spelled alike. I'm going to show you what I mean with Jesse's example. Jesse, you said that that <u>see</u> and <u>me</u> are rhyming words. Do they sound alike?

Class: Yes.

Miss Moser: Yes. But look at them. Look at the way they are spelled. What do you notice?

John: That <u>see</u> has two <u>e</u>s and <u>me</u> has only one <u>e</u>.

Miss Moser: Right. So the spelling pattern, or word family, at the end is spelled differently. Today as you listen to the story, you are going to search for rhyming words. Then we have to decide if those rhyming words have the same word family or different word families. First listen to the story.

After listening and discussing the story:

Miss Moser: Now we are going to read the story again.

Class: "See that squirrel in our tree? I think he'd rather live with me."

Miss Moser: What do you notice? Which words rhyme?

Anna: *Tree* and *me*?

Miss Moser: *Tree* and *me*. Can you point to them in our book here? Good. Now let's add them to our chart. Anna said <u>tree</u> and <u>me</u>. Which column do I have to fill in here? Jesse, do you want to help her out? Do they have the same word family or a different one?

Jesse: They are different.

Miss Moser: They are different. So we'll put a check in this column that says Different Word Families. And what should we write on these lines here?

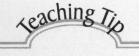

Jesse: Double *e* and one *e*?

Miss Moser: You got it!

Lesson Modifications

Provide extra support: Spend more time in the beginning of the lesson talking about rhyming words that are spelled differently. Generate several examples for each word family, such as *high, thigh, sigh* and *my, sky, try, dry, by*.

Provide a challenge: Revisit the text a third time. Using Cover-up Labeling Tape, have the students identify the spelling of the covered rime in one rhyming word per page.

Spelling-Pattern Activities

1. **What Looks Right?** In this activity, students learn to use their visual memory to select the correct spelling for words. On an overhead projector or the board, label two columns with words that rhyme but are spelled differently, such as *coat* and *vote*. Have the students copy the columns and words on their own paper. Now say a word that rhymes with *coat* and *vote* and write it with both spellings. For example, say, "If *goat* is spelled like *coat*, it will be g-o-a-t. If *goat* is spelled like *vote*, it will be g-o-t-e." Write *goat* and *gote* and ask students which way looks right. They then write the word in the column that they think is correct and check their decision with a dictionary. On the board, cross out the spellings that are found to be incorrect, and continue with other examples.

   From *Making Words* by Patricia M. Cunningham and D.P. Hall.

2. **Sort the Spelling Patterns.** Brainstorm a long list of words that all share the same sound, such as long *i* words (*night, by, buy, bite, kite, high, eye, slide, sky, fight, kind, find, tie, my,* and *sigh*). Now categorize the words according to their spelling rule (*igh, i, y, eye, uy, i* with silent *e,* and *ie.*)

More Books for Teaching Spelling Patterns

Bears by Ruth Krauss (Scholastic Trade, 1993). This lightly worded book describes b*ears* under st*airs* and b*ears* giving st*ares*; b*ears* who are million*aires* and b*ears* who are everywh*eres*! Big Book.

Madeline by Ludwig Bemelmans (Puffin Books, 1998). This classic story of a brave little girl's trip to the hospital is filled with silent *e* words: "In an old house in Paris that was covered with vines lived twelve little girls in two straight lines." Big Book.

Altoona Baboona by Janie Bynum (Harcourt Brace, 1999). This perky story about the adventures of Altoona Baboona's journey in a "hot-air balloon-a" is packed with *oo* words.

Rhyming Words and How They Are Spelled

Rhyming Words		Same Word Family	Different Word Families
_____	_____	☐ Word Family _____	☐ Word Families _____ and _____
_____	_____	☐ Word Family _____	☐ Word Families _____ and _____
_____	_____	☐ Word Family _____	☐ Word Families _____ and _____
_____	_____	☐ Word Family _____	☐ Word Families _____ and _____
_____	_____	☐ Word Family _____	☐ Word Families _____ and _____
_____	_____	☐ Word Family _____	☐ Word Families _____ and _____
_____	_____	☐ Word Family _____	☐ Word Families _____ and _____
_____	_____	☐ Word Family _____	☐ Word Families _____ and _____
_____	_____	☐ Word Family _____	☐ Word Families _____ and _____
_____	_____	☐ Word Family _____	☐ Word Families _____ and _____
_____	_____	☐ Word Family _____	☐ Word Families _____ and _____
_____	_____	☐ Word Family _____	☐ Word Families _____ and _____
_____	_____	☐ Word Family _____	☐ Word Families _____ and _____
_____	_____	☐ Word Family _____	☐ Word Families _____ and _____

Teaching the Essentials of Reading With Picture Books Scholastic Teaching Resources

Chapter 3

Fluency

No longer the forgotten reading component (at least not in this book), fluency is the ability to read text quickly, accurately, smoothly, and with comprehension. What better way to practice fluency than with portions of easy-to-read picture books that kids are excited to read?

The key to effective fluency instruction is to model fluent reading while also explaining why you have emphasized particular words or phrases, why you have read at varying speeds, and why you clumped certain words together. Of course, practice in the form of repeated readings is also crucial. The following lessons provide a guideline for talking about fluency as well as motivating repeated reading activities.

Improve Reading Fluency

Teach Students to

Improve phrasing and intonation

Use punctuation signals

Read dialogue

With Picture Books

The Wind Blew by Pat Hutchins

The Little Mouse, the Red Ripe Strawberry, and the Big Hungry Bear by Don and Audrey Wood

Andrew's Loose Tooth by Robert Munsch

Modeling Phrasing and Intonation

With *The Wind Blew* by Pat Hutchins

Presented by Jennifer Gibbons and her first-grade class

Fluency is the reading component that gets the least attention (Allington, 1983). The problem is that if students are not able to read text quickly, accurately, and smoothly, their comprehension suffers (Nathan and Stanovich, 1991). Some students who are not fluent readers spend most of their energy decoding words, leaving little energy left for comprehending. Other students read words accurately, but it is their poor phrasing and intonation that hampers their comprehension (Rasinski, 2003). This lesson addresses the needs of the second type of student.

One of the most powerful ways to help students become fluent readers is to model fluent reading and explain why we emphasize particular words or phrases (*intonation*), read at varying speeds (*rate*), and clump certain words together (*phrasing*) (Rasinski and Padak, 2001). Reading specialist Jennifer Gibbons begins her fluency lesson with a mini-lesson. The mini-lesson helps her students realize that we don't always need an obvious signal, like a question mark or exclamation point, to read with expression. She begins with *The Wind Blew* because of its simple sentences and limited punctuation. As the book has only five commas and a period ending each sentence, she can model the effect that intonation and phrasing have on the way a story sounds, and how the sound affects the story's meaning.

The Wind Blew is an engaging adventure about the day the wind blew and whisked away everything in its path. The rhythmic language, repetitive structure, and rhyme further support children's fluency and make this book a good choice for echo reading. Echo reading is an effective fluency activity in which the teacher reads a phrase or sentence of the story and the children echo the reading.

LESSON

Phrasing and Intonation Mini-Lesson

Before reading, give a brief demonstration of how the same sentence sounds different when you read it at different speeds, emphasize different words, and vary the tone of your voice. Write the following sentence on the chalkboard or chart paper: "Matt loves meatballs." As you read the sentence, emphasize a different word each time, pointing to that word as you read.

> *Matt* loves meatballs.
>
> Matt *loves* meatballs.
>
> Matt loves *meatballs*.

Ask the students whether they heard the difference in the way the sentence was read. Talk about how emphasizing different words changes the focus in the sentence. In *Matt loves meatballs*, we are meant to focus on the fact that it is Matt, and not someone else, who loves meatballs. In *Matt **loves** meatballs*, we are meant to understand that Matt is really, really fond of meatballs. In *Matt loves **meatballs***, we are meant to focus on the fact that it is meatballs, not another kind of food, that Matt finds delicious.

Now read the sentence slowly and in a monotone. Then read it naturally, as if you were talking to a friend. Do they hear the difference in the way the sentence was read? Which way did they like you to read it?

Try reading the sentence, or parts of it, quickly and slowly, high pitched and low pitched. Repeat this process with a couple of sentences that you create before reading the story. Explain that reading with expression not only makes reading more interesting, it is also easier to understand what we read. Sometimes, it is the reader's job to figure out *how* the author wants us to read the sentences.

❑ On the first reading, read *The Wind Blew* for pleasure.

❑ Before rereading *The Wind Blew,* set the purpose for reading: *to listen to how the story is read and to read it with the same expression.* Explain to the class that after you read a sentence, they will read the sentence the same way.

❑ Pages in this story are not numbered, so I have assigned 1 to the page that reads, "The wind blew." As you read this sentence, stretch out the word *blew* for emphasis. Talk about how you read the sentence and what you did to make the words interesting. Point to each word as you read the sentence again and ask the students to read the sentence just as you did.

❑ On page 3, read, "It took the umbrella from Mr. White *(with a slight pause)* and quickly *(read quickly)* turned it inside OUT." Did the students notice any difference in your voice? What else can they say about the way you read the sentence? Did they notice where you paused? Did they notice which words you emphasized? Point to each word as you read the sentence again and have the class echo what you read.

❑ From time to time, read a sentence in a monotone before reading it with expression. Talk about how reading with expression brings out the story's meaning: the way the words are read goes logically with what the words mean.

❑ Repeat the process with the rest of the story.

LESSON IN ACTION

Ms. Gibbons: Listen to how I read the first sentence of the story: "The wind bleeeew." What did you notice about the way I read that sentence?

Kimberly: You made the word <u>blew</u> sound long.

Ms. Gibbons: That's right. I stretched out the sounds in the word. Why do you think I did that?

Otobo: To make the story more interesting.

Ms. Gibbons: True, I wanted to make the words sound interesting. But why do you think I chose to read the word _blew_ the way I did?

Walter: Maybe to sort of sound like the wind?

Ms. Gibbons: You got it! How does the wind sound when it blows?

Class: _Whhhhhhhhh_.

Ms. Gibbons: Now say "bleeeeeeew."

Class: _Bleeeeeeew_.

Ms. Gibbons: When we stretch out the sounds in the word _blew_, it sounds a little like the stretched out sound of wind blowing. Now we can more easily picture the windy, windy day that is described in this story.

Denise: I think reading _blew_ like _bleeeeew_ tells that it is really, really, really windy.

Ms. Gibbons: Great point! Look at this picture. This isn't just a breezy day. This looks like a very, very windy day. And if I read you this first sentence the way that I did, but I didn't show you the picture, you would have a better understanding that the wind was a strong wind. Listen to the way I read the sentence once again, and then you echo the way I read it: "The wind bleeeew."

Class: "The wind bleeeew."

Ms. Gibbons: Good. Let's try the next sentence. "It took the umbrella from Mr. White (_pause_) and quickly (_read quickly_) turned it inside out." Did I read this entire page in one breath?

Joshua: Yes.

Ms. Gibbons: I did? Listen again. Can anyone tell me where I paused, or took a little rest?

Tonisha: After you read "Mr. White."

Ms. Gibbons: Yes! Why do you think we did that?

Aaron: Because the sentence is on two lines?

Ms. Gibbons: Yes, this sentence is certainly a longer sentence than "The wind blew." Take a look at this word here (_pointing to and_). Sometimes when we see the word _and_, we pause right before it because we know that there is more sentence to come. Now listen to me read the sentence again. Which word did I read quickly?

Jason: _Quickly_.

Ms. Gibbons: Why do you think I read _quickly_ quickly?

Destiny: Because you wanted to sort of say it like it happened quickly.

Ms. Gibbons: Yes. When we emphasize certain words, we emphasize what they mean, too. When we read the word _quickly_ fast, we are saying that the wind is really fast and swift. I'm going to read the sentence once more, and you echo how I read it.

Lesson Modifications

Provide extra support: The sentences in this story can easily be broken in two parts, making echo reading easier for students. You can also read and echo-read each sentence twice for extra support and practice.

Provide a challenge: Experiment with more than one way to read the sentence. Students may also enjoy being leaders and having the class echo the way they read the sentence.

Teacher-Guided Fluency Activities

❏ **Echo Reading:** Model reading a phrase or sentence with fluency, then have students repeat what you read and how you read it. Modifications of echo reading include creating an audiotape that has pauses after phrases and sentences to allow for student participation. You can also have students be echo leaders, if they are familiar with the text and demonstrate good fluency.

❏ **Choral Reading:** Students and teacher read all or parts of the text in unison. Like echo reading, choral reading is great for shy readers who are not ready to perform on their own. Choral reading can be done many ways, including: 1) unison reading of a refrain; 2) unison reading of an entire text; and 3) assigning text to two or more groups. Ideal text choices for choral reading are poems; books that are predictable, repetitive, or rhyming; and books with a refrain.

❏ **One-on-One Reading:** Students need lots of opportunities to practice reading material at or below their reading level. When students read to a teacher or another adult, they receive immediate feedback and encouragement. Help students select an appropriate book or text. After they have practiced reading the text several times, have them read to you or another adult. An interested audience of one provides both motivation and instruction.

See page 50 for fluency practice activities for individuals and peer partners.

Fluency Takes Practice, Practice, Practice!

Students need a great deal of practice reading easy-reading books to become fluent themselves (Samuels, Schermer, and Reinking, 1992). Easy-reader series provide an opportunity for your students to get to know characters and different writers' styles. Here are some suggested resources.

Easy-Reader Series

Curious George books by H.A. Rey and Margret Rey

Frog and Toad books by Arnold Lobel

George and Martha books by James Marshall

Henry and Mudge books by Cynthia Rylant

Little Bear books by Else Minarik

More Reading Materials for Building Fluency

poetry

repetitive text

predictable text

chants and songs

More Books for Modeling Phrasing and Intonation

Sheep on a Ship by Nancy Shaw (Houghton Mifflin, 1989). How much expression and excitement can children bring to these simple, rhyming sentences that describe a ship of sheep that sail into a storm? "Winds whip. Sails rip. Sheep can't sail their sagging ship."

Sometimes I Feel Like a Mouse: A Book About Feelings by Jeanne Modesitt (Scholastic, 1992). The content of the sentences and supporting illustrations in this predictable book solicit unique intonation for each sentence: "Sometimes I feel like a swan floating calm. Sometimes I feel like a lion roaring mad."

Clifford the Big Red Dog by Norman Bridwell (Scholastic, 1985). This story about the hugely popular Clifford is told in simple language. Big Book.

Teaching the Power of Punctuation

With *The Little Mouse, the Red Ripe Strawberry, and the Big Hungry Bear* by Don and Audrey Wood

Presented by Jennifer Gibbons with her second-grade class

In the previous lesson, students learned how to use phrasing and intonation to read with expression and convey meaning. In this lesson, students learn how punctuation marks and other typographical signals, such as bold print, italics, enlarged print, and underlining, affect meaning and, therefore, the way they read the text.

A lesson about punctuation and typographical signals requires an exciting book with lots of fun examples. That's why reading specialist Jennifer Gibbons chose *The Little Mouse, the Red Ripe Strawberry, and the Big Hungry Bear* to teach this fluency lesson. This story about how the little Mouse does his very best to hide a strawberry from the big, hungry Bear is loaded with commas, question marks, and exclamation points, as well as words in capital letters for emphasis. Jennifer models and explains how her pacing, phrasing, and intonation change throughout the story, as dictated by the punctuation.

LESSON

Punctuation and Typography Mini-Lesson

Before reading the story, give a brief mini-lesson on specific punctuation marks and typographical signals and what they mean. First, invite students to tell you what they do when they see the following signals as they read:

- comma (pause)
- period (longer pause)
- question mark (raise your voice at the end of the sentence)
- exclamation point (read with strong feelings of joy, fear, anger, horror, or surprise)
- words that are underlined, bold, italicized, large, small, or all capitals (stress these words)

Put selected student responses in a large chart that shows the typographical signal and its name, what the signal means, and a sentence containing the signal. Students can add to the chart as new signals are encountered.

Next, put the signals into action. Use the sentences below or similar sentences to demonstrate how meaning changes when different signals are used.

I love meatballs.

I love meatballs!

I love meatballs?

I love MEATBALLS!

I <u>love</u> meatballs.

I love meatballs.

After you read each sentence, talk about how the signals affected how you read the sentence. How did the meaning of the sentence change? Can they tell you how you should read a sentence you point to before you read it? Have volunteers take turns reading the sentences and explaining why they read the sentence as they did. Explain that paying attention to these signals not only makes a story more interesting, it also makes the story easier to understand because, as they now see, the signals also affect the meaning of the sentence.

❑ Read and discuss *The Little Mouse, the Red Ripe Strawberry, and the Big Hungry Bear* for fun.

❑ Before you reread the story as a "think-aloud," set the purpose for reading: *to notice the punctuation in the story and listen to how the punctuation tells the reader how to read the sentences.*

❑ Tell the class you want them to be on the lookout for the signals you just discussed and to think about why the authors used the signals. The pages in this book are not numbered, so I have assigned 1 to the page that reads "Hello, little Mouse. What are you doing?" After reading this page, ask the students if they notice anything different about the two sentences (one sentence ends in a period, the other in a question mark). Why did the authors put the question mark after the second sentence? Can the students tell you how you made the second sentence sound like a question? Could they detect your pause at the comma in the first sentence?

❑ On page 8 you'll find an ellipsis. Explain that the authors used this signal because they want the reader to pause or slow down. It is similar to a comma, but even stronger. Now would be a good time to add ellipsis to the signals chart.

❑ Continue locating the signals throughout the story, stopping to discuss how they affect the way the text is read, and how they help the reader understand the story by showing the author's intended meaning.

LESSON IN ACTION

Ms. Gibbons: (_Points to the words_ "BOOM! BOOM! BOOM!" _on page 12_.) Why do you think the authors put these words like this, in all capital letters?

Walter: Because you are supposed to go, "BOOM! BOOM! BOOM!" (_read with great emphasis_).

Ms. Gibbons: Yes, they want you to read these words with lots of expression and feeling. They not only put an exclamation mark after the words, but they also used all capital letters, and if we look back at our signals chart, we see that when words are written in all capitals, we are supposed to stress those words. Where else on this page are capital letters used to tell us to stress the words?

Jose: "SNIFF! SNIFF! SNIFF!"

Ms. Gibbons: Right. So now let's think about why the author wants us to emphasize these particular words, and not other words on this page. Remember, the signals on the page tell us how to read the words, but they also help us understand the story better. Listen as I read: "BOOM! BOOM! BOOM! The Bear will tromp through the forest on his big, hungry feet, and SNIFF! SNIFF! SNIFF! find the strawberry . . ." Who in the story is doing the booming and the sniffing?

Destiny: The bear.

Ms. Gibbons: Yes. And what do we know about this bear?

Jackie: He is big and hungry.

Ms. Gibbons: Absolutely. He is big and hungry. So what do the authors want us to know about the way this bear is booming and sniffing?

Melvin: I think that because the bear is so much bigger than the mouse, the authors made the words for the bear bigger, too.

Ms. Gibbons: That makes sense to me. The authors are letting us know that when this bear tromps through the forest, he makes a big sound because he is a big bear. Someone else?

Joshua: His nose is so big that when he sniffs, it makes a really loud sound.

Ms. Gibbons: Good point. The big bear probably makes a lot of noise when he sniffs because he is so big. And maybe because he is really hungry, he is sniffing louder than if he weren't so hungry. "BOOM! BOOM! BOOM!" and "SNIFF! SNIFF! SNIFF!" help us understand just how big and hungry the bear is. Let's imagine for a minute that in this story, the little mouse didn't eat the strawberry, but he ran through the forest to get away from the bear. Do you think the authors would use the words *BOOM! BOOM! BOOM!* to describe how the mouse sounds running through the forest?

Class: No!!!

Ms. Gibbons: I don't think so either. That wouldn't really make sense. A mouse is so small, it wouldn't be capable of making that much noise. So when authors use punctuation marks and other signals, they help us to better understand the meaning of words and the meaning of the story.

Lesson Modifications

Provide extra support: Make the author's choice of question marks and exclamation points more obvious by covering them up and replacing them with different punctuation marks. Talk about how these changes affect meaning.

Provide a challenge: Read through the story with the punctuation marks covered with sticky notes. Ask students to identify appropriate punctuation marks for the end of those sentences.

Independent and Partner Fluency Activities

☐ **Tape-Assisted Reading:** Audiobooks provide students with a new and exciting voice to model fluency with their favorite books. Listening to a new voice can be very motivating. As students listen to a story on tape (one written at their instructional level or below), they read along with the same text. When they read along silently, they improve their comprehension, word recognition skills, and overall fluency. Students can also read aloud with the tape, as they would in choral reading. For a wonderfully authentic reason to practice and perform, students can make their own book on tape. A student-made audiobook makes a wonderful gift for, say, a kindergarten class.

☐ **Partner Reading:** Partner reading is essentially a one-on-one tutorial between two students. A less fluent reader can be paired with a fluent reader. The fluent reader can be a peer or an older student. First, the stronger reader models fluent reading with a page or paragraph of text. The less fluent reader then reads the text. The fluent reader provides assistance when needed, as well as feedback and encouragement. The less fluent reader rereads the text until it is read accurately and with fluency. Partners of the same ability can take turns reading text that has previously been read in a teacher-guided lesson.

Reading Performances: One of the most effective and motivating ways for children to improve their fluency is by reading to an interested audience. A performance requires practice, practice, practice, and the payoff is extremely concrete and satisfying. We've already discussed students making a book on tape for an audience. Students can also read a story to a younger audience or select poems to share. Reader's Theater is another great vehicle for reading performances, and is discussed in detail on page 54.

See page 45 for teacher-guided fluency practice.

More Books to Teach the Power of Punctuation

If You Take a Mouse to School by Laura Numeroff (Laura Geringer Books, 2002). As children read about Mouse's requests that never seem to end, they'll encounter powerful and predictably located commas: "If you take a mouse to school, he'll ask you for your lunch box. When you give him your lunch box, he'll want a sandwich to go with it."

How Do Dinosaurs Get Well Soon? By Jane Yolen (Blue Sky Press, 2003). "What if a dinosaur catches the flu? Does he whimper and whine in between each Atchoo?" What a wonderful way to learn or review question marks! There are 16 in this rhyming book. This book is also a great choice for choral reading.

Suddenly! By Colin McNaughton (Harcourt Brace, 1995). "Preston was walking home from school one day when suddenly!" This is a story about a wolf that comes close to having Preston the pig for lunch, but never succeeds. Almost every page of simple text ends with *suddenly!* A real thriller, this book ensures that each exclamation will be read with gusto.

Modeling Dialogue

With *Andrew's Loose Tooth* by Robert Munsch

Presented by Jamie Levine and her second-grade class

Good readers read dialogue as they think the character might say the words. They tune in to the story events and the character's feelings and convey meaning through expression and intonation. Conversely, poor readers often miss or misinterpret the author's intended meaning because they lack fluency and read in a monotonous, word-by-word manner (Opitz and Rasinski, 1998). In the following lesson, Jamie Levine models how to read dialogue the way she thinks the character would say the words. She then solicits ideas from the students about why she read the dialogue the way that she does, referring to information from the story, clue words, pictures, punctuation marks, and other typographical signals, as well as her prior knowledge.

Andrew's Loose Tooth is a favorite in Jamie's class. The children rally behind Andrew, whose loose tooth causes him pain and distress. Things only get worse when his parents, the dentist, his friend Louis, and the Tooth Fairy come up with outrageous ways to get that tooth out. The dialogue is funny and charged with emotion, which makes for an energized lesson on thinking about how characters would sound if they could talk.

LESSON

❑ Read *Andrew's Loose Tooth* aloud for pleasure. Before rereading the story, set the purpose for reading: *to listen to how the character's words are read and think about why the words are read that way.*

❑ After reading the dialogue on page 2 with a great deal of expression, point to the word "YEEE-OW!" and ask students why they think you read this word the way that you did. There are many sources of information to discuss: 1) Andrew yelled "YEEE-OW!" because it hurt when he bit into the apple with a loose tooth; 2) the word *yelled* before "YEEE-OW!" is a clue word that tells the reader to actually say the word loudly; 3) "YEEE-OW!" is written in all capital letters, the print is bold, and there is an exclamation point at the end—all signals to read the word with lots of expression and emotion; 4) prior knowledge of biting into food with a loose tooth might lead one to read "YEEE-OW!" with lots of emphasis and emotion; and 5) the picture shows Andrew screaming and jumping in pain. Have the students tell you what you did with your voice to show that Andrew is in pain. Can they think about a time when they stubbed their toe or felt a sudden pain? What did they sound like when they spoke? What was their voice like?

◻ Reread the rest of Andrew's dialogue on page 2 quickly and with urgency: "Mommy, Mommy! Do something about this tooth. It hurts so much I can't even eat my apple." Ask the class why you read these sentences quickly, not slowly? Reread the entire dialogue in a slow, bored, monotone manner and compare the two readings. In addition to the fact that the story is not nearly as enjoyable to listen to when read the second way, talk about how the monotonous reading makes it hard to understand the story. It actually doesn't make sense that someone who is in pain would speak in a slow and bored way, so to read the story this way is confusing and not the way the author intended the story to be read.

◻ Continue reading the story in this manner, stopping to ask students why you are reading the dialogue the way that you are. Point out that there are many ways authors let us know how to read dialogue, such as with punctuation and other typographical signals, clue words, and pictures. But sometimes the author doesn't give us clues, and we have to really think about what is happening in the story and what the character might be feeling in order to know how to read the character's words.

LESSON IN ACTION

After reading page 18:

Mrs. Levine: How would you describe the way I read Andrew's words on this page: " 'Oh,' " said Andrew, 'My mother can't get this tooth out. My father can't get this tooth out. The dentist can't get this tooth out. And I can't eat my breakfast.' "

Jeremy: Sad.

Mrs. Levine: Why do you think I made Andrew sound sad here? Elsa?

Elsa: Because Andrew is sad that he can't eat his breakfast.

Mrs. Levine: Yes. Why else is he sad?

Elsa: Nobody can get his tooth out!

Mrs. Levine: Okay. So we know that he is sad because he says himself that his mother, his father, and his dentist can't get his tooth out, and as a result, he can't even eat his breakfast! Does anybody see another clue on the page that lets me know how to read Andrew's words?

Beth: It says that Andrew looked very sad.

Mrs. Levine: Excellent! Here the author is telling us in the paragraph before that Andrew sat in the front yard looking sad, and when Louis asks what's the matter, Andrew explains why he is sad. Good. Rodger?

Rodger: Andrew looks sad in the picture.

Mrs. Levine: There's another clue! Good eyes, Rodger. So there are many ways that we know that Andrew is sad. Who can tell me what I did with my voice to show that Andrew is sad? Pilar?

Pilar: You read really slowly, like you were feeling really down.

Mrs. Levine: Uh-huh. I read slowly, like I was frustrated and out of steam. I even whined a little bit, right? Can you understand how Andrew feels in this situation?

Class: Yes!

Lesson Modifications

Provide extra support: Begin the lesson with specific examples of the author giving readers clues about how characters feel through pictures, punctuation, typographical symbols, and word choice.

Provide a challenge: Read a piece of dialogue with inappropriate phrasing, intonation, and expression. Do the children believe that the character would have said the words in the same way? How do they think the character would say the words?

Performing Dialogue With Reader's Theater

Excerpted from "The Power of Reader's Theater," by Jennifer O. Prescott, *Instructor*, January/February 2003.

"If you want to get your kids reading with comprehension, expression, fluency, and joy," says children's book specialist and *Instructor* columnist Judy Freeman, "there's nothing more effective than Reader's Theater. Beyond its efficacy, the best news about Reader's Theater is how easy it can be. In Reader's Theater, students read from scripts as they stand in front of their audience. It does not require extensive preparation, fancy costumes, props, sets, or memorization."

Jo Worthy, a former classroom teacher and currently an associate professor of education at the University of Texas, explains that Reader's Theater "is a pretty controlled way of doing drama, so it's especially nice for the shy student or teacher. You have a script in front of you—kind of nice to hide behind—and that gives you security." Students take turns reading their lines with as much creative expression as they can. It's that simple. However, students need to be aware of one another and to listen respectfully.

Reader's Theater in Five Easy Steps

1. **Choose a script.** Choose a prepared script, or have students choose a book from which to develop a Reader's Theater script.

2. **Adapt the script.** If adapting, have students identify speaking parts (including narrators) and break down the story into dialogue.

3. **Assign parts.** Students might try out different parts to get a feel for them, then choose their roles themselves.

4. **Highlight parts and rehearse.** Students highlight their dialogue, then practice their lines at home and in groups during school.

5. **Perform.** The cast reads the play aloud for an audience, often made up of parents or younger students.

More Books for Modeling Dialogue

Alligator Baby by Robert Munsch (Scholastic Books, 2002). There is never a dull moment in this hysterically funny book about a new addition to the family. Kids will love to jump in and express the emotions of the exasperated family members: Kristen lifted up the middle of the blanket, saw a green claw and said, "That's not a people claw!"

Owl Babies by Martin Waddell (Candlewick Press, 1992). Three baby owls worry about the whereabouts of their mother. There are over 20 opportunities for students to read the expressive one-liners from anxious Sarah, Percy, and Bill.

Folktales such as "The Little Red Hen" and "The Three Billy Goats Gruff" are good choices for modeling and independent reading practice. These stories also make great Reader's Theater scripts. Both are available in Big Book format from Scholastic.

Teaching Tip

Reader's Theater Resources

Books

15 Easy-to-Read Mini-Plays (K–2), by Sheryl Ann Crawford and Nancy I. Sanders (Scholastic, 2002).

Folk Tale Plays from Around the World That Kids Will Love!, by Marci Appelbaum and Jeff Catanese (Scholastic, 2002).

Readers Theatre for Beginning Readers (Grades 1–4), by Suzanne I. Barchers (Teacher Ideas Press, 1993).

Free Scripts!

These and other sites offer scripts that are free for classroom use. One caveat: Public performances of many scripts and book adaptations require publisher's or author's permission.

www.aaronshep.com

www.readinglady.com

www.loiswalker.com

www.storycart.com

www.lisablau.com

Chapter 4

Vocabulary

One of my favorite aspects of teaching was to instill a love of words and share the tools for unlocking the meaning of unknown words. The teachers featured in this section love vocabulary building as well.

Invite students to be word sleuths as they strategically uncover the meanings of unfamiliar words in their favorite picture books and beyond.

Building Vocabulary

Teach Students to

Learn specific words and concepts

Use word parts

Use context clues

With Picture Books

The Foolish Tortoise by Richard Buckley

A House for Hermit Crab by Eric Carle

Stellaluna by Janell Cannon

Teaching Specific Words and Concepts

With *The Foolish Tortoise* by Richard Buckley

Presented by Diane Marzigliano and her second-grade class

Children learn most vocabulary indirectly through conversations with others, read-alouds, and by reading on their own. Yet some vocabulary must be taught directly. When specific words that represent difficult concepts are taught before a book is read, students' comprehension increases. For optimal learning, follow up the initial vocabulary instruction with repeated exposure to the new words. Provide opportunities for students to use words in different contexts that reinforce their meaning.

Diane chose *The Foolish Tortoise* to teach the concept of foolishness. Understanding of this concept is important to understanding the story plot. While many students are acquainted with the concept, Diane's lesson will clarify and enrich the meaning. This lesson may even inspire students to make *foolish* part of their speaking vocabulary! This rhyming story is about a tortoise that makes a foolish choice and suffers for it. Each of Eric Carle's brightly illustrated pages depicts the consequences of the foolish act and the tortoise's deep regret. Diane uses a concept web during reading to introduce foolishness and pull out examples and consequences of the concept from the text.

LESSON

Pre-reading

Make a transparency or enlarged replication of the concept web on page 60. When you first introduce the concept web, cover the bottom half ("Identify the foolish act" and "Eight consequences of the foolish act").

Write "foolish" in the box on the web labeled "Word." Ask students if they recognize a smaller word in *foolish* (*fool*). Ask volunteers to define the word *fool* (a person who is not smart or is unwise). Be sure that students understand the meaning of *unwise*. Now ask volunteers to define *foolish*. Record appropriate responses on the concept web in the box labeled "Meaning" and explain that *foolish* is a word used to describe someone or something unwise, or not smart. Invite students to give examples of someone acting in a foolish way. Next, ask a volunteer to use the word *foolish* in a sentence and record the sentence on the concept web.

❑ Present *The Foolish Tortoise* and inform students that the tortoise in the story does something that is very foolish. Encourage students to predict what that might be. Then read the book straight through for pleasure.

□ On the second reading, set the purpose for reading: *to listen for and record the tortoise's foolish act and the consequences of the foolish act.*

□ Tell students that this time as you read, you will stop at certain points to talk about what is happening in the book and complete the concept web. Because the pages of this book are not numbered, I have assigned 1 to the first page of story text.

□ Read through page 4 and stop to ask the class what the tortoise did on this page. Ask why they think the tortoise took off his shell. Do they think it was a wise or foolish decision for the tortoise to take off his shell? After filling in the "Identify the foolish act" box on the concept web, tell students that the last part of the concept web asks for eight consequences of the foolish act, or what happens to the tortoise because of the foolish act.

□ After reading page 5, ask students what they think the author means by "Though faster, he was not express and his protection was far less." How did this lack of protection make the tortoise feel? Talk about how hiding beneath a stone and behind a tree and feeling "weak behind the knees" are two consequences of taking off the shell. Fill in two turtles on the concept web with these examples.

□ Continue to discuss and record the consequences throughout the story. Pages 8 through 17 reveal six more consequences of the foolish act: not feeling safe (page 8), almost being eaten by a snake (page 10), no longer having shade (page 14), getting soaked to the skin (page 14), shivering with cold (page 16), and losing the urge to roam (page 17). When you reach the end, ask the students whether they think the tortoise was wise or foolish to return to his shell. Why or why not?

□ Remember to revisit the concept of foolishness over the coming months and provide opportunities for students to use the word in different contexts to help solidify their understanding of the concept.

Here is what our concept web looks like. You may select different consequences and wording.

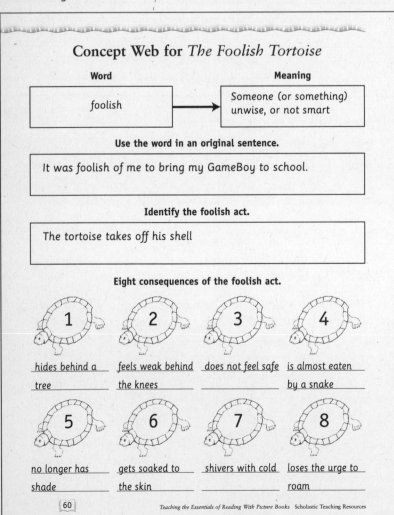

Concept Web for *The Foolish Tortoise*

Word
foolish

→

Meaning
Someone (or something) unwise, or not smart

Use the word in an original sentence.

It was foolish of me to bring my GameBoy to school.

Identify the foolish act.

The tortoise takes off his shell

Eight consequences of the foolish act.

1. hides behind a tree
2. feels weak behind the knees
3. does not feel safe
4. is almost eaten by a snake
5. no longer has shade
6. gets soaked to the skin
7. shivers with cold
8. loses the urge to roam

Teaching the Essentials of Reading With Picture Books Scholastic Teaching Resources

LESSON IN ACTION ....

After reading page 14:

Ms. Marzigliano: Janelle?

Janelle: If he had his shell he would have gone inside and he wouldn't have gotten soaked to the skin.

Ms. Marzigliano: Did you hear what she said? Janelle explained a consequence very well. She said that if the tortoise had had his shell, he would have gone inside and he wouldn't have gotten soaked to the skin. So what do we notice here? What is happening? Ashley?

Ashley: When he wants shade, the sun comes up, and when he doesn't want to get soaked, the rain comes down. If he had his shell, he wouldn't have to worry.

Ms. Marzigliano: Excellent! If he had had his shell, he would have been protected from the hot sun and the rain. Look at all these consequences he has to face now because he did a very . . .

Class: foolish thing!!

Lesson Modifications

Provide extra support: On sentence strips, write examples of wise and foolish acts. Have students categorize these acts into two separate columns labeled "Foolish" and "Wise."

Provide a challenge: Have students work independently to create their own sentences describing wise and foolish acts. Then have students share their wise and foolish ideas with a partner and categorize the acts into two separate columns labeled "Foolish" and "Wise."

More Books for Teaching Specific Concepts

Wilfrid Gordon McDonald Partridge by Mem Fox (Kane/Miller Book Publishers, 1985). Wilfrid lives next to a nursing home. When he learns that his favorite friend, Miss Nancy, has lost her memory, he realizes that he doesn't know what a memory is!

The Good Luck Cat by Joy Harjo (Harcourt Brace, 2000) and *Lucky Bear* by Joan Phillips (Random House, 1986). Here are two books for teaching the concept of luck. The first book is a story of a cat's nine lives. The second book is an easy reader that flips back and forth between a lucky situation (Lucky me. Here is a boat.) and an unlucky outcome (Oh no! It is sinking!).

Becoming Butterflies by Anne Rockwell (Walker & Company, 2002). Don't forget to use nonfiction picture books to teach vocabulary for complex concepts. Explore the concept of metamorphosis with this story about a teacher who brings caterpillars and milkweed to school. Her students watch with amazement as the wormy creatures turn into beautiful butterflies.

Concept Web for *The Foolish Tortoise*

Word

Meaning

Use the word in an original sentence.

Identify the foolish act.

Eight consequences of the foolish act.

1

2

3

4

_____

_____

_____

_____

5

6

7

8

_____

_____

_____

_____

Teaching the Essentials of Reading With Picture Books Scholastic Teaching Resources

Additional Word and Concept Webs

Here are more webs to use when teaching new words and concepts.

Some Word Meanings

Word

What it means.

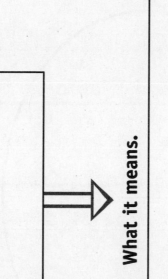

These are some examples.

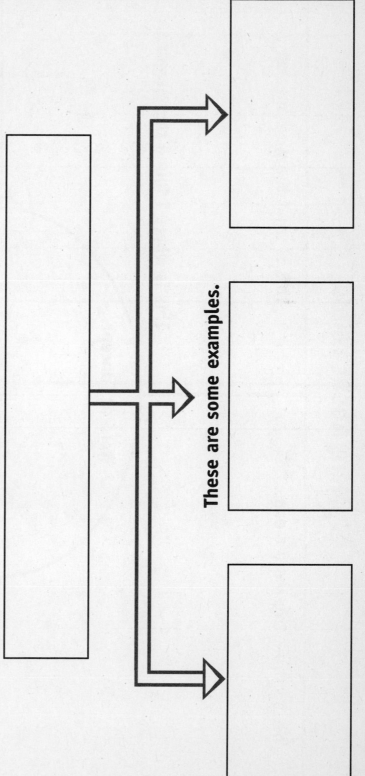

More About Words

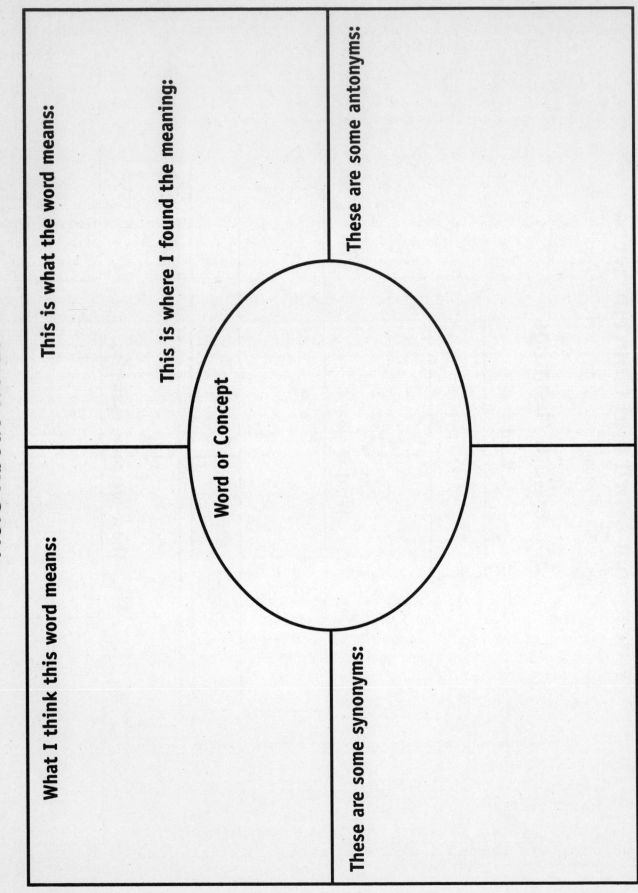

This is what the word means:

This is where I found the meaning:

These are some antonyms:

What I think this word means:

Word or Concept

These are some synonyms:

Teaching Word Parts

With *A House for Hermit Crab* by Eric Carle

Presented by Randy Gangnes and her first-and-second-grade class

As students' reading vocabularies expand, they begin to encounter longer, more complex words. It becomes increasingly important for readers to learn to recognize familiar word parts within longer words. Direct instruction in base words, prefixes, and suffixes helps young readers learn the meaning of many new words. Students use their understanding of how prefixes and suffixes affect the meaning of the base word to infer the meaning of the longer word. Direct instruction in common prefixes and suffixes also gives students the tools to figure out the meaning of hundreds of other words with the same prefixes and suffixes.

Randy Gangnes chose to focus on suffixes because suffixes occur much more frequently in text written for young readers than do prefixes and are thus a better investment in learning (Fox, 2000). She selected *A House for Hermit Crab* by Eric Carle because of the frequency and predictable location of *-ly* words. This book tells the story of a hermit crab who invites a variety of helpful and attractive sea creatures to decorate his shell home. The author consistently uses adverbs with the suffixes *-ly* to describe the actions of the hermit crab as he places the decorations on his shell. The focus of Randy's lesson is to explore the meanings of base words and remind the children that when *-ly* is added to a word, it tells how something is being done.

LESSON

Advance Preparation

Place removable highlighting tape over the vocabulary words on which this lesson will focus (*Gently* on page 6, *Carefully* on page 8, *Gingerly* on page 10, *Happily* on page 12, and *Gratefully* on page 14). Note: Because the pages of this book are not numbered, I have assigned 1 to the first page containing text.

Other materials you should have ready include:

- a pocket chart
- five cards with these base words: *gentle, careful, happy, grateful,* and *ginger*
- five cards with the suffix *-ly*
- one card with the letter *i*

Note: It would be best to use one color for the base word cards and another color for the suffix and letter *i* cards.

☐ Read the story to the class. Students will notice the highlighting tape and be curious about its function, but for now take advantage of their curiosity and assure them that they will soon find out why the tape is there. Challenge them to begin thinking about why the tape might be there.

☐ On the second reading, set the purpose for reading: *to learn how the word ending* -ly *changes the meaning of the base word.*

☐ Tell students that they will now try to discover why some of the words in this story have been highlighted. Students will notice on page 4 that *gently* is one of these special words. Ask them if this word reminds them of any other word they've heard. Someone should say *gentle*. Place the *gentle* word card in the pocket chart. Ask them what it means. Then ask, "How has the word *gentle* been changed into *gently*?" Place the suffix card -*ly* over the -*le* of *gentle* and say, "Yes, an ending, or a *suffix*, has been added to the word. The word *gentle* could describe the hermit crab (the hermit crab is very gentle), but the word *gently* describes *how* the hermit crab picked up the sea anemone."

☐ The process will be the same for *carefully*, the second highlighted word on page 6. When you ask if *carefully* reminds them of another word they know, *careful* should be mentioned, although *care* might also be brought up. At this point, it will make more sense to work with *careful*.

☐ *Gingerly* on page 8 is a more difficult word to discuss because the base word, *ginger*, will probably be unfamiliar. You may want them to find its meaning through context, since it is very similar to *gentle*, and *careful*, and also tells *how*, or the manner in which, the hermit crab picked up the coral.

☐ On page 10, the highlighted word is *happily*. Again, ask students if it reminds them of a more familiar word. When *happy* is mentioned, place the base word card in the pocket chart. Ask how *happy* has been changed to *happily*. Lead them to realize that the *y* in *happy* has been changed to *i* before the suffix -*ly* was added. Place the *i* card over the *y*. Say, "The hermit crab is happy. *Happily* tells *how* the hermit crab picked up the snail."

☐ Continue through the story in the same manner, using your cards to demonstrate how the suffix -*ly* has been added to base words. Discuss the meanings of the base words and remind the students that when -*ly* is added to a word, it tells *how*, or the way, something is being done.

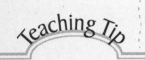

Teaching Tip

Share these steps with your students to help them dissect a word with a suffix:

Look for a suffix.

Peel it off.

Do you see a word that you know?

Read the word.

What does it mean?

From *Word Identification Strategies* by Barbara J. Fox

Lesson Modifications

Provide extra support: This book also has many words with the suffixes *-s*, *-ed*, and *-ing*. These suffixes are commonly found in literature for young children and may be an easier place to start with younger or less experienced readers.

Provide a challenge: For more advanced learners, you can extend the lesson by focusing on the words in the story to which the suffix *-y* has been added (*gloomy, murky, spiky*). You could use these words to further extend the concept of changing *y* to *i* before adding a suffix, guiding students toward forming *gloomily* and *murkily*.

Activities That Familiarize Students With Word Parts

1. **Word-Ending Flowers:**
   Create a chart or overhead transparency of a flower with six petals. In the center of the flower, write a base word to which suffixes, prefixes, or both can be added, such as *care, hope,* or *appear*. Can students think of words that have the same base word, such as *cares, careful, careless, carefree, caring,* and *cared*?

   Write one word per petal. Talk about how the prefix or suffix affects the meaning of each word. Then invite students to use each new word in a sentence. Write the sentence under the word in the petal.

2. **I Spy Word Parts:** Write words that have a variety of word parts on cards and put them on a wall. Play *I Spy* with your word wall: *I spy a word that ends in* -ly a*nd begins with an* s (slowly). *I spy two words that have the base word* agree (disagree, agreeable).

3. **Word-Part Riddles:** Help children learn the meaning of prefixes and suffixes with riddles: *I am in the words* disappear, disagree, *and* disinterested. *I don't mean many, but I do mean not* (dis).

The 20 Most Common Prefixes

PART	MEANING
un	not, opposite of
re	again
in, im, ir, ill	not
dis	not, opposite of
en, em	cause to
non	not
in, im	in or into
over	too much
mis	wrongly
sub	under
pre	before
inter	between, among
fore	before
de	opposite of
trans	across
super	above
semi	half
anti	against
mid	middle
under	too little

The 20 Most Common Suffixes

PART	MEANING
s, es	plurals
ed	past-tense verbs
ing	verb form/present participle
ly	characteristic of
er, or	person connected with
ion, tion, ation, ition	act, process
ible, able	can be done
al, ial	having characteristics of
y	characterized by
ness	state of, condition of
ity, ty	state of
ment	action or process
ic	having characteristics of
ous, eous, ious	possessing the qualities of
en	made of
er	comparative
ive, ative, itive	adjective form of noun
ful	full of
less	without
est	comparative

From *Phonics from A to Z: A Practical Guide* by Wiley Blevins, Scholastic, 1998.

More Books for Teaching Word Parts

What's Up, What's Down? by Lola M. Schaefer (Greenwillow Books, 2002). With this imaginative book, students explore the world from many perspectives and come across a slew of wonderfully descriptive words ending in *-ing*.

The Grouchy Ladybug by Eric Carle (HarperCollins, 1996). While looking for a fight, the grouchy ladybug rejects each animal because she does not believe them to be big enough. But they are all ready to oblige: "If you insist, said the stag beetle, opening its jaw. If you insist, said the praying mantis, reaching out with its long front legs."

An Extraordinary Egg by Leo Lionni (Scholastic, 1994). A little frog discovers an extraordinary egg on Pebble Island. Your students will discover the meaning of many *extra*ordinary words by looking at roots and suffixes, such as *midsummer*, *reappeared*, and *inseparable*. Big Book.

Using Context Clues

With *Stellaluna* by Janell Cannon

Presented by Peggy Hayes and her second-grade class

The development of a rich vocabulary plays an important role in reading comprehension. Comprehension cannot be attained if the reader doesn't know the meaning of many of the words in a text. Students learn most word meanings indirectly, or from context. Therefore, it is important that they learn to use context clues effectively (Nagy and Herman, 1987). Context clues are hints about the meaning of an unknown word that are rendered in the words, phrases, and sentences that surround that word. How many times have we, as adults, determined the meaning of a challenging word by finding a clue in a phrase, a comparison, or an additional sentence that clarifies the meaning for us? Particularly in pleasure reading, stopping to use a dictionary may divert our attention and in other instances it is just not practical. One of the best ways to help students develop their ability to use context clues is through modeling. Think-alouds during the shared reading of big books and read-alouds enable teachers to demonstrate how to use this valuable strategy.

Literacy staff developer Peggy Hayes chose *Stellaluna* for a lesson on using context clues because it is a word-rich story loved by children and teachers alike. In this touching story about a bat that lives temporarily with a family of birds, students encounter a number of challenging words, but the meanings are embedded in context clues. Peggy begins with a mini-lesson on what to do when we come to a word we don't know and proceeds to model how to find and use context clues.

LESSON

Pre-Reading

Determine the vocabulary you'd like to teach. Four to six words make for a good lesson, but you may want to teach more or fewer depending on the needs of your class. The following story words are good choices for teaching context clues: *sultry* (page 1), *clutched* (page 1), *swooped* (page 3), *dodging* (page 3), *shrieking* (page 3), *limp* (page 3), *trembling* (page 3), *clambered* (page 5), *gripping* (page 11), *anxious* (page 23), *survived* (page 31), *gasped* (page 29), *grasped* (page 30), and *limb* (page 39). Note: The pages in the book are not numbered, so I have assigned 1 to the first page of text.

Ask students what they do when they come to a word they don't know the meaning of. Write their responses on chart paper. Responses might include: *ask the teacher what the word means, skip over the word and keep reading, use a dictionary, look for clues in the picture, make a guess and see if it makes sense*. Explain that some of these are great strategies for figuring out a word they don't know. Today, they are going to practice some of the strategies, particularly how to find and use clues in the story to figure out unknown words. Make an overhead transparency from the bookmark reproducible on page 73 and discuss how to find clues.

Provide students with copies of the **When You Come to a Word You Don't Know the Meaning of . . .** bookmark and talk about each step. Refer to the steps throughout the lesson.

Explain that this book has many hard words. Since you want to understand what the words mean, you will stop at points in the story and ask the class to use the strategies to help you figure out the hard words. Thinking out loud and using clues to figure out what words mean will help you understand the entire story.

Before, during, and after the reading of this book be particularly aware of the vocabulary choices of the students in their comments. Celebrate the wise choice of words whenever this opportunity arises.

Finding Clues to Help Figure Out an Unknown Word

1. Clues can be found in pictures and in words.

2. Clues in the text can be one word, a few words, or a sentence.

3. Clues in the text can be a definition, restatement, example, or description.

Example: The twins *pondered* the plans for their birthday party. The more they thought about it, the more they wanted a beach party.

The clue is in the second sentence. "The more they thought about it" makes it sound as if they continued to ponder. In fact, ponder means to think about something carefully. So in this case, the clue is actually a definition.

❑ Set the purpose for rereading *Stellaluna*: *to use clues in the story to figure out what difficult words mean.*

❑ Begin reading, stopping at the end of the page to discuss predetermined vocabulary words. The first sentence reads: "In a warm and *sultry* forest far, far away, there once lived a mother fruit bat and her new baby." Express your confusion about the meaning of the word *sultry*. Can the students find a word in that sentence that might be a clue (*warm*)? Ask students what happens when it is warm? We feel hot and sweaty or sticky. The air can be humid. Substitute the word *humid* or *sticky* for *sultry* in the sentence. Ask

---

When You Come to a Word You Don't Know the Meaning of . . .

1. Skip the word and keep reading to the end of the sentence. Were there any clues in the sentence?

2. If not, look for clues in the words, phrases, or sentences that come before and after the unknown word.

3. Look for clues in the picture.

4. Use the clues to make a guess about what the hard word means.

5. Replace the unknown word with your guess. If the sentence makes sense, read on. If the sentence doesn't make sense, try again.

students if that sounds right and makes sense. Congratulate them on using a context clue to determine a word meaning.

> NOTE: *Explain to students that clues about a word's meaning are not always helpful. Although you may have led them through the line of thinking that produced* humid, *any number of words would make sense in place of* sultry, *such as breezy, fragrant, pleasant, or quiet. Clues in the text are helpful but not a sure thing, as is a dictionary definition. Why use clues in the text if they don't always give us the meaning of hard words? Because they often help us understand hard words, and we do not always have a dictionary handy when we read.*

❏ The end of the first page reads "Each night, Mother Bat would carry Stellaluna *clutched* to her breast as she flew out to search for food." Which word or words act as clues (*carry, breast, flew*)? Point out that if Mother Bat is carrying her baby as she flies, then she needs to hold her close to her body. She also needs to hold on tightly, which is what the word *clutched* means. Substitute *held tightly* to confirm that this choice makes sense.

❏ These are just a few of the many ways in which context clues may be used to determine the meaning of unknown words. Continue to read, stopping after reading a page where challenging words are encountered.

LESSON IN ACTION

Mrs. Hayes: Here is another word that I want you to look at very, very carefully: "Her baby wings were as *limp* and useless as wet paper." What does the word *limp* mean? *Limp*.

David: Tiny?

Mrs. Hayes: Something can be limp and be tiny, but it doesn't have to be tiny to be limp. I've seen big things that were limp, too. I see something in the sentence that can help us tremendously. "Her baby wings were as *limp* and useless as . . ." Whenever I see the word *as* followed by the word *as* again a few words later, that gives me a clue that I am comparing two things. What did the author compare the wings to?

Eugene: Wet paper.

Mrs. Hayes: Wet paper! I want you to think for a second about wet paper. How is paper when it is wet? That will tell us what *limp* means because the author made a comparison.

Gabrielle: It's soggy.

Mrs. Hayes: Good. What else is it?

Ashley: The paper gets wet and soaked.

Teaching the Essentials of Reading With Picture Books   Scholastic Teaching Resources

Mrs. Hayes: And what happens to the paper once that happens? What does it look like? How is it different?

Patrick: It could be really weak and when you pick it up and go like that, it will just start to break.

Mrs. Hayes: What was the first word you used, "It could be really . . ."

Patrick: Weak.

Mrs. Hayes: Weak. Wet paper is weak and floppy and rips easily. It is not firm or strong. Let's replace _limp_ with our new words and see if they sound right. "Her baby wings were as _weak_ and useless as wet paper." Does this make sense?

Class: Yes!

Mrs. Hayes: "Her baby wings were as _floppy_ and useless as wet paper." Does this make sense?

Class: Yes!

Mrs. Hayes: Way to use those context clues!

Lesson Modifications

Provide extra support: Prior to teaching the _Stellaluna_ lesson, have students practice replacing known words with other words that make sense. Cover selected words in a favorite picture book and help students use semantic and syntactic clues to come up with other word choices that do not change the meaning of the sentence.

Provide a challenge: For students with a large vocabulary and an understanding of how to use context clues, invite them to lead a think-aloud with a vocabulary word in the story accompanied by helpful context clues. Guide them as needed.

Context Clue Activities

1. **Play With Homophones.** After presenting a mini-lesson on homophones, have students brainstorm as many homophones as they can and record their responses on the board or chart paper. Divide the class into partners. Each pair of students gets a piece of paper that has a pair of homophones written on the top. The partners co-write a sentence for each homophone. Check that the homophones are used correctly before covering the homophones with a sticky note. Then have the partners exchange their paper with another set of partners. The students write the correct homophone on the sticky note, then lift the sticky note to see if they used the homophone correctly. What clues helped them decide which word to use?

2. **Complete Cloze Activities.** Have students practice using context clues with cloze procedures in which every fifth to seventh word in a reading passage is omitted. Students must rely in part on context clues to successfully complete the activity.

3. **Create a Context Clues Poster.** Find or write examples in which a variety of context clues are demonstrated in a variety of places (in the same sentence as the challenging word, in the preceding sentence, in the following sentence, or in a few sentences before or after the word). Highlight the context clue(s) in each example and refer to the poster to remind students how to find clues as they read.

More Books for Teaching Context Clues

Antarctica by Helen Cowcher (Farrar, Straus and Giroux, 1990). This beautifully illustrated nonfiction book describes the daily activities and dangers shared by animals of Antarctica. Context clues are provided for *mate, huddles, lurks, trudges,* and *ancient.* Big Book.

The Woman Who Outshone the Sun from a poem by Alejandro Cruz Martinez (Children's Book Press, 1991). When Lucia Zenteno arrives in town, the villagers don't know what to make of her ability to soak up the river water with her hair and comb it out again. After they mistreat the mysterious girl, the villagers learn to treat her with kindness, even though she is different from them. Vocabulary includes *outshone, glorious, honored, refused,* and *cruel.* Big Book.

Mission to Mars by Franklyn M. Branley (HarperCollins Publishers, 2002). This read-aloud illustrated science picture book has useful context clues for the words *launched, recover, transfer, recycled,* and more.

When You Come to a Word You Don't Know the Meaning of . . .

1. Skip the word and keep reading to the end of the sentence. Were there any clues in the sentence?

2. If not, look for clues in the words, phrases, or sentences that come before and after the unknown word.

3. Look for clues in the picture.

4. Use the clues to make a guess about what the hard word means.

5. Replace the unknown word with your guess. If the sentence makes sense, read on. If the sentence doesn't make sense, try again.

Chapter 5

Reading Comprehension

Of course, text comprehension is the reason we read in the first place. Without comprehension, reading is simply an exercise in sounding out words.

Comprehension instruction with favorite picture books takes advantage of the fact that students are naturally motivated by the book and have a strong desire to understand the story. In this section, the following comprehension strategies are expertly modeled.

Building Comprehension Skills

Teach Students to		With Picture Books
Use graphic organizers		*How Puppies Grow* by Millicent Selsam
Use question-answer relationships		*Jamaica's Find* by Juanita Havill
Summarize		*The Mitten* by Jan Brett

Using Graphic Organizers

With *How Puppies Grow* by Millicent E. Selsam

Presented by Peggy Hayes and her first-grade class

Graphic organizers are visual diagrams that help students organize, interpret, and understand material. They come in many shapes and forms, and target many types of information. (See pages 80–82 for sample graphic organizers.) Graphic organizers can be used with any type of text, from informational to narrative. In fact, these organizational tools help students become aware of the structure of the text they are reading.

In the following lesson, literacy staff developer Peggy Hayes guides students to pull information from a nonfiction text and place the information in a sequencing graphic organizer. She chose *How Puppies Grow* because of the clear, sequential description of changes a puppy goes through over time. *How Puppies Grow* is also one of her favorite nonfiction texts. Her students are fascinated with the book as well. Puppies are an all-time favorite topic for children, and the appealing photos really hold their attention. The clear organizational pattern of events and the motivating topic set the stage for an engaging lesson on using a graphic organizer to show sequence.

LESSON

❑ Prior to reading *How Puppies Grow,* ask students if they have a pet at home. Then ask how many of them have a dog. Did they get the dog when it was a puppy? Draw attention to the fact that owning a puppy and an older dog can be somewhat different in the beginning. Elicit from students what happens to puppies over time.

❑ Take a "picture-walk" through the book and encourage students to identify the nonfiction genre, which is characterized by photographs and facts. How long do they think it took for the puppies to go through the changes? Hours? Days? Weeks? Years? Guide their responses and support their sense of time with examples.

❑ Read the book aloud for enjoyment. Point out references to specific changes that the puppies experience and when they take place.

❑ Now set the purpose for reading: *to listen for specific examples of how and when the puppies change, and to put this information on a chart.*

❑ Make an overhead transparency or enlarged version of the graphic organizer on page 79. Walk students through the

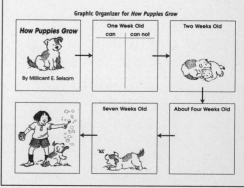

graphic organizer and explain the chart's purpose: to show how a puppy grows over time.

❑ As you read the book, pause after each page and ask students if there is any information that you just read that needs to be recorded on the chart. Continue to the end of the book.

LESSON IN ACTION

Introduction

Mrs. Hayes: We know this is a book about puppies, and it isn't make-believe. It is true. So if it isn't make-believe, and the information in here is true, what kind of book is it?

Destiny: Nonfiction.

Mrs. Hayes: Oh, you need to scream that out! I am so proud of you.

Destiny: Nonfiction!

Mrs. Hayes: Nonfiction books have lots of facts in them. And when I read a book with lots of facts in it, I need to get the facts organized in my head. I like to use a chart like this to keep all the facts together because I don't want them all over the place. I don't want to mix up facts about a puppy with facts about a grown-up dog. So the first time I read this, I want you to listen very carefully. Let me see you open your ears, shape them good. As I read, I would like you to see what happens when the puppy is one week old—what it can do and what it can't do. Then when it is two weeks old . . . watch where the arrows are going . . . about four weeks, and then I am moving to about seven weeks. During the first reading you are listening, you are thinking. The second time, we are going to fill in this chart with the information in this book. Did you know that this chart is called a _graphic organizer_? Those are very grown-up words, but a graphic organizer helps us organize information. Here we go.

Conclusion

Mrs. Hayes: Why is it good to have something like this graphic organizer when we read? How does that help you?

Justin: It is teaching the dog how to learn stuff.

Mrs. Hayes: Is it teaching the dog how to learn stuff? I think I am learning something from this when I look at it. What did you learn from this graphic organizer?

Roxanne: It helps you to remember everything.

Mrs. Hayes: Yes! It helps you remember information, and also to put the information in the right . . .

Class: Order.

Mrs. Hayes: That's right. Because if I look at this chart, I say, "When the puppy is first born, that's a good time for him to be a pet." Am I right or wrong?

Class: Wrong!

Mrs. Hayes: Wrong, because that's not what happens in the beginning. That happens at the . . .

Class: End!

Mrs. Hayes: At the end. This chart is good because it helps me organize information by time. Other graphic organizers help me tell a story with a beginning, middle, or end, or compare two characters. There are lots of ways to organize information with graphic organizers. You all did a beautiful, beautiful job. Thank you very much!

Lesson Modifications

Provide extra support: Some students may have difficulty with the concept of the passing of time. It may be necessary to review how many days there are in a week and about how many weeks make a month. This could be included in a cross-curriculum lesson in mathematics.

Provide a challenge: Have students refer to the completed graphic organizer to write a summary of *How Puppies Grow*.

More Books to Use with Graphic Organizers

A Color of His Own by Leo Lionni (Delmar Publishers, 1990). Use a graphic organizer to identify the beginning, middle, and end of this story about a chameleon who searches for a color all his own.

Sheila Rae, the Brave by Kevin Henkes (Greenwillow Books, 1987). When Sheila Rae is too brave for her own good, her sister saves the day. Use a character graphic organizer to organize the many examples of how Sheila Rae is brave.

The Three Little Pigs by Steven Kellogg (HarperCollins Publishers, 1997). You'll need a super-sized Venn diagram to capture how Kellogg's version of "The Three Little Pigs" compares to the classic, but your students will have a ball sorting through all the terrific details.

Graphic Organizer for *How Puppies Grow*

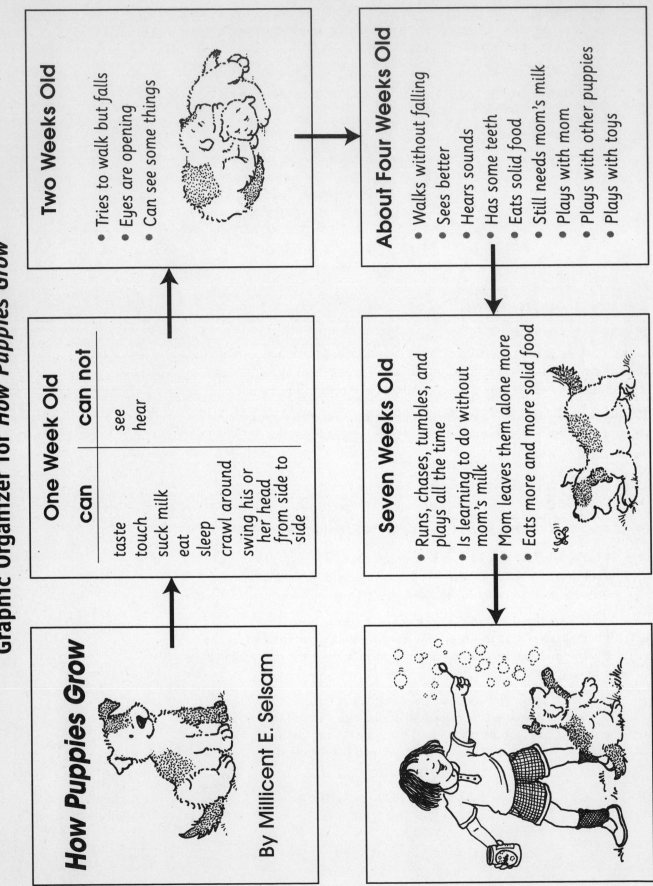

How Puppies Grow

By Millicent E. Selsam

One Week Old

can	can not
taste	see
touch	hear
suck milk	
eat	
sleep	
crawl around	
swing his or her head from side to side	

Two Weeks Old

- Tries to walk but falls
- Eyes are opening
- Can see some things

About Four Weeks Old

- Walks without falling
- Sees better
- Hears sounds
- Has some teeth
- Eats solid food
- Still needs mom's milk
- Plays with mom
- Plays with other puppies
- Plays with toys

Seven Weeks Old

- Runs, chases, tumbles, and plays all the time
- Is learning to do without mom's milk
- Mom leaves them alone more
- Eats more and more solid food

Teaching the Essentials of Reading With Picture Books Scholastic Teaching Resources

Graphic Organizer for *How Puppies Grow*

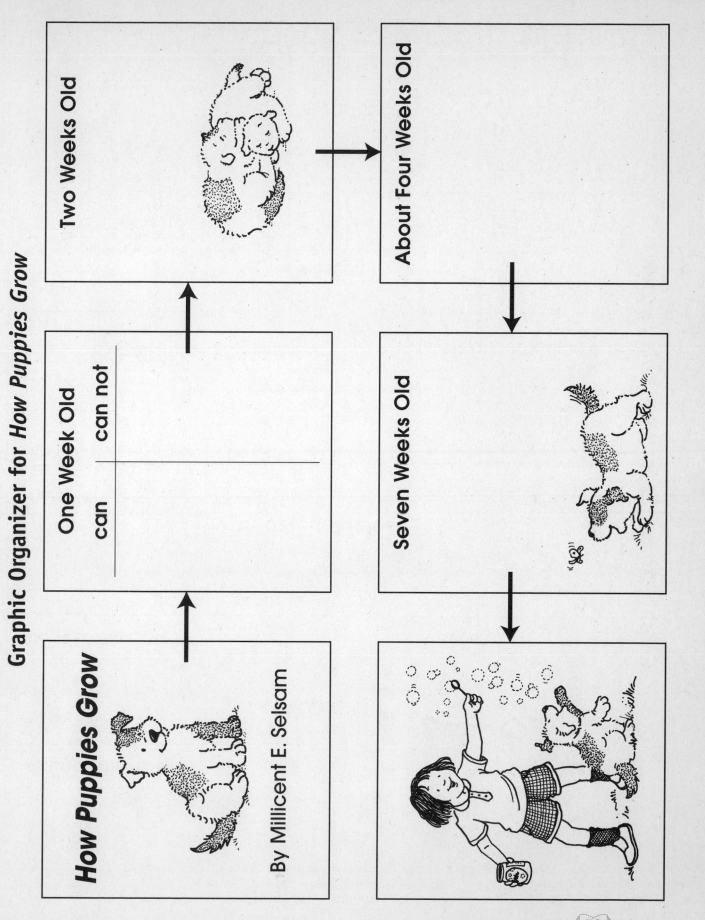

How Puppies Grow

By Millicent E. Selsam

One Week Old

can | can not

Two Weeks Old

About Four Weeks Old

Seven Weeks Old

Six Graphic Organizers to Strengthen Comprehension

Story Map

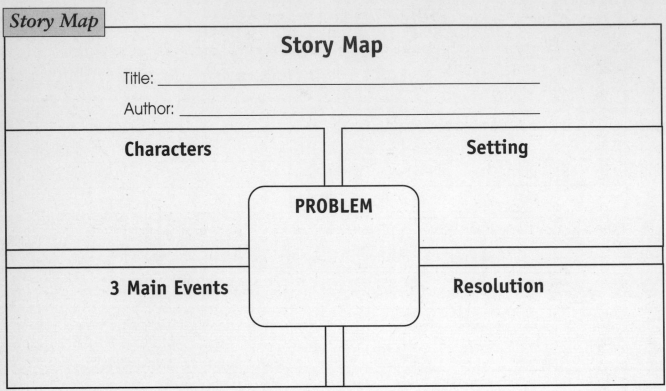

Story Map

Title: _____

Author: _____

Characters	Setting

PROBLEM

3 Main Events	Resolution

Adapted from *Easy Reading Lessons for the Overhead* by Lisa Blau, Scholastic Professional Books

Character Map

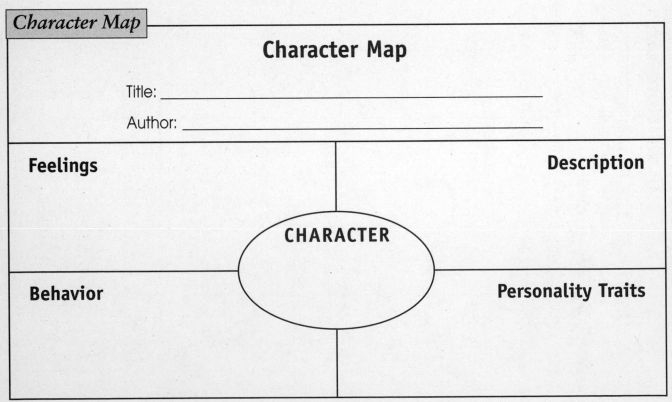

Character Map

Title: _____

Author: _____

Feelings	Description

CHARACTER

Behavior	Personality Traits

Adapted from *Easy Reading Lessons for the Overhead* by Lisa Blau, Scholastic Professional Books

Cause and Effect

Why Did It Happen?

Think about an event or a character's action that you read about. Then write what happened as a result of this.

This is the title of what I read: _____

This is the **cause** statement:	Here are the **effects**:
_____	_____
_____	_____
_____	
Draw a picture to show the **cause**.	Draw a picture to show one **effect**.

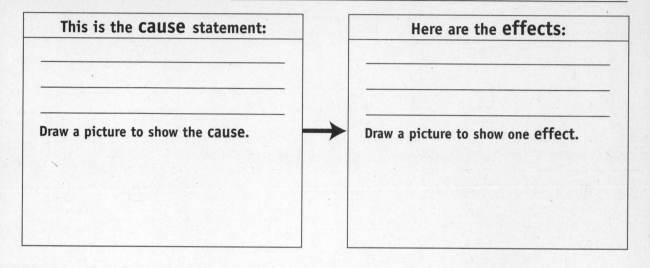

Adapted from *Scholastic News Learn-Along*, 2000

Sequencing

Tell the Story

In what order did the events happen?   Topic: _____

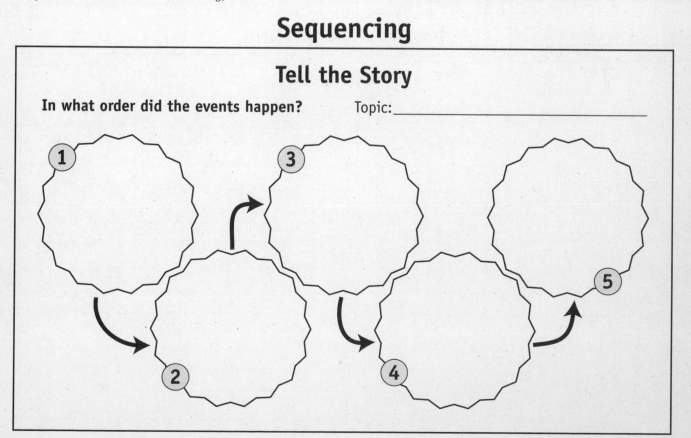

Summarizing

Retell the Story

Write details from a story, using the 5 W's chart below.

The 5 W's

1. Who _____
2. What _____
3. Where _____
4. When _____
5. Why _____

Now tell the story in your own words. Use the 5 W's to help you.

_____

_____

_____

Adapted from *Scholastic News Learn-Along*, 2000

Posing Questions

My Questions

Write down questions you have before, during, and after reading.

1. This is a question I had before I read:

   _____

   _____

   _____

2. This is a question I had while I was reading:

   _____

   _____

3. This is a question I had after I read:

   _____

   _____

   _____

Adapted from *Scholastic News*, 2001

Teaching Question-Answer Relationships

With *Jamaica's Find* by Juanita Havill

Presented by Peggy Hayes and her second-grade class

The average teacher asks students hundreds of questions every day. Questioning aids in text comprehension because it helps students read with a purpose, think actively as they read, monitor their comprehension, review what they read, and make connections between what they read and what they already know. Although questioning is a useful assessment tool, we can make this comprehension strategy more effective when we vary the types of questions we ask. We can also teach children to understand where the answers to those questions are found. In this lesson, children learn that answers can be found in the following ways: right there (answer is clearly stated in a sentence); think and search (answer is implied and found in two or more sentences); and on your own (answer comes from the reader's background and prior knowledge, not the text).

Jamaica's Find by Juanita Havill provides the opportunity for a diverse level of questioning. The main character, Jamaica, finds something that is not hers, but she would really like to keep it anyway. Literacy staff developer Peggy Hayes chose this book because, like most teachers, she witnesses children who are confronted with a similar dilemma. This is a story with depth that children can definitely relate to, making *Jamaica's Find* a great choice for exploring question-answer relationships.

LESSON

Day 1: Question-Answer Relationship Mini-Lesson

Before reading *Jamaica's Find*, pre-teach the three types of answers. Provide examples of each type of answer with a short reading passage, such as the one found on page 89 titled *Meet Jane Yolen*. In a think-aloud model, show students how you determine answers to questions, and identify where the answers are found.

❏ Make a transparency of *Meet Jane Yolen* or make copies for each student. Make a copy of the question cards found on page 88 and cut out the six cards.

❏ Before reading the passage, explain that Jane Yolen is a famous children's author. Then read the passage.

❏ Now hand out the numbered question cards to six students. After each student reads a question, answer the question. Be sure that students ask the questions in order.

Here is how the lesson may look:

RIGHT-THERE ANSWER

Student asks
question #1: What is a "green" person according to Jane Yolen?

Mrs. Hayes: A "green" person is someone who loves nature.

Student asks
question #2: What kind of answer is this? Why?

Mrs. Hayes: This is a _right-there_ answer. The author says what a "green" person is here in the second sentence. (_Point to and read the sentence._)

THINK-AND-SEARCH ANSWER

Student asks
question #3: What is the author talking about when she tells of the "swee-swash" of wind or the "kee-ya" of a hawk?

Mrs. Hayes: They are the sounds the wind and a hawk make.

Student asks
question #4: What kind of answer is this?

Mrs. Hayes: This is a _think-and-search_ answer because the author doesn't come out and say that the wind sounds like "swee-swash" or that a hawk says "kee-ya." But she tells us to listen to them, so we know they are sounds. The words "of the wind" and "of a hawk" tell us that these are the sounds that the wind and a hawk make.

ON-YOUR-OWN ANSWER

Student asks
question #5: What color word might you use to describe someone who is angry? How about someone who is sad? Can you explain why?

Mrs. Hayes: Someone who is angry might be described as being red because sometimes people's faces get red when they are angry. Someone who is sad might be described as being blue because sometimes we say a person is feeling blue when they are sad.

Student asks
question #6: What kind of answer is this and why?

Mrs. Hayes: This is an _on-your-own_ answer because the answer isn't in the author's words. You have to think of your own answer. I sometimes feel my face getting hot and red when I am really angry. I sometimes ask my daughter if she is feeling blue when she looks unhappy.

Day 2: *Read* Jamaica's Find

Present *Jamaica's Find* as a read-aloud and think-along to a group of students. Before you begin to read, set the purpose: *to better understand the story by answering questions about it and to identify where the answers were found (right there, think and search, or on your own).*

❑ As you present the cover, ask, "What do you think Jamaica found? Why do you think that?" Tell students to see if their prediction is correct as you read on.

❑ Read through page 8. Have the students confirm or revise their predictions. Ask, "Was this stuffed dog brand new or old? Can you tell me how you knew this?" Think-and-search: "It was old. It was worn from hugging; faded food and grass stains were all over it and its nose was off." (See second paragraph on page 8.)

❑ Read pages 10–15. Ask, "Why didn't Jamaica return the dog with the hat?" Think-and-search: "She liked the dog and wanted to keep it. She wanted to take it home." (See page 15.)

❑ Ask: "When Jamaica's mom said, 'Maybe the dog doesn't fit you either,' what did she mean?" On-your-own: "The dog wasn't hers to keep either, just like the hat."

❑ Read pages 16–19. Ask, "What could Jamaica be thinking as she looked closely at the dog?" On-your-own: "Should I keep you or not? I wonder what the girl who lost the dog is feeling."

❑ Read pages 20–23. Ask, "What decision did Jamaica make while she was in her bedroom?" Right-there: "She decided to bring the dog back to the park." (See the last two lines on page 23.)

The questions in this lesson serve as examples and can easily be modified or substituted for.

LESSON IN ACTION

Mrs. Hayes: In yesterday's lesson we talked about three different types of questions that we might be asked after we read something. Can anyone share with us what you learned about the questions?

Jelessa: A right-there question is the easiest.

Mrs. Hayes: What makes you say that?

Jelessa: Well, we call it right-there because you can find the exact answer in the story. The author sort of gives it to you like a present.

Mrs. Hayes: That's excellent, and you remembered how we compare it to a gift that is given. What are the other two kinds of questions?

Louis: Well, there is the think-and-search, which is a little harder because the author doesn't exactly tell you and you have to figure it out using story clues. The other kind is answered on your own.

Mrs. Hayes: What helps you to answer an on-your-own question?

Denise: You have to use things that you know or learned that are not in the book to figure out the answer. That's a harder kind of question.

Mrs. Hayes: As I read _Jamaica's Find_, I will be stopping and asking questions as I go along. Why do you think teachers do that?

David: They want to see if you're paying attention.

Mrs. Hayes: That's true. Would there be any other reason?

Regina: Maybe it will help you to understand the story.

Mrs. Hayes: Excellent. As I ask questions about what I read, you can be my reading detectives. What will you be doing?

Louis: We'll be listening for clues to help us answer the questions.

After reading page 8:

Mrs. Hayes: Did Jamaica find a new or an old stuffed dog?

Kiara: It was really old.

Mrs. Hayes: Can someone be a reading detective and tell us the clues that helped Kiara to answer this question correctly?

Nigel: Well it didn't exactly say that it was an old dog, so it wasn't a right-there answer, but I heard you read that the dog was faded and it had food and grass stains and the nose fell off, so it can't be too new.

Mrs. Hayes: Reading detective Nigel, you are absolutely right! You had to think and search for those clues.

Lesson Modifications

Provide extra support: In cases where prior knowledge is limited, help to "fill in the blanks" and build some background information. For example, after reading the expression "Jamaica was feeling hot around her ears" on page 24, explain that sometimes our body shows how we are really feeling. Ask students if they have ever felt hot and red in the ears and face when they are embarrassed. Talk about why Jamaica may have felt embarrassed.

Provide a challenge: Give your higher-level students the opportunity to share their question-answer relationship skills with struggling classmates. They can take on the role of teacher in a whole-class or small-group setting and share where they find the answers to questions, while you offer support and clarification as necessary.

Generating Questions

The flip side of answering questions is asking questions. When we teach students to ask their own questions as they read, we help them actively engage in their reading. When students ask questions, they also become aware of whether or not they understand what they read. Here's an activity to help students generate their own questions with another book in Juanita Havill's *Jamaica* series.

Either with a small group or the whole class, prepare students for a read-aloud and think-aloud session. Explain that they will now take on the active role of thinking out loud and asking questions as you read aloud the book *Jamaica and the Substitute Teacher*. Tell children that good readers ask themselves questions as they read because it helps them understand the story better.

While reading the book, stop at predetermined points to take questions from the children. In addition to discussing the questions and possible answers, have the children identify their questions as being right there, think and search, or on your own.

Suggested think-aloud points in the text:

- ❑ after the third page, where clues are given about a hidden object
- ❑ following the math lesson and exchange about cats
- ❑ after the marking of the spelling test
- ❑ at the conclusion of the book, after Jamaica admits that she copied

More Books for Teaching Question-Answer Relationships

A Chair for My Mother by Vera B. Williams (Greenwillow Books, 1982). After losing their furniture in a fire, a young girl and her mother save all their coins in a jar. Finally, they have enough money to buy a big, soft armchair. This touching story provides lots of real-life situations and emotions to explore with questions. Big Book.

Angelina on Stage by Katherine Holabird (Pleasant Company Publications, 2001). Angelina and Henry have parts in a grown-ups' ballet. There are many questions to raise when Angelina's excitement turns to jealousy.

Doctor De Soto by William Steig (Farrar, Straus and Giroux, 1997). This story about a clever mouse-dentist who outwits a hungry fox with a toothache is a fun book to discuss and explore.

Question Cards for Question-Answer Relationship Mini-Lesson

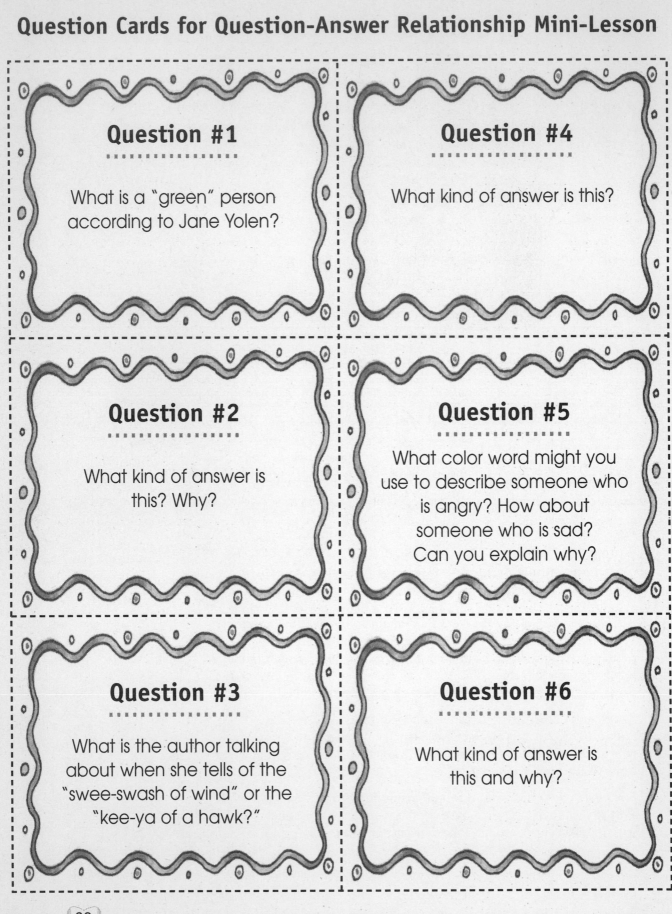

Question #1

What is a "green" person according to Jane Yolen?

Question #2

What kind of answer is this? Why?

Question #3

What is the author talking about when she tells of the "swee-swash of wind" or the "kee-ya of a hawk?"

Question #4

What kind of answer is this?

Question #5

What color word might you use to describe someone who is angry? How about someone who is sad? Can you explain why?

Question #6

What kind of answer is this and why?

Meet Jane Yolen

I think of myself as a "green" person. A "green" person is someone who loves nature. I have written many nature books. My book *Color Me a Rhyme* is a poetry book about nature's many colors.

Writing Tip: To write "color poems," find something in nature. Go out and sit in a meadow or park. Feel the grass beneath you. Watch the sky overhead. Listen to the swee-swash of wind through reeds, the kee-ya of a hawk. Become a tree, a flower, a fern uncurling in spring.

Adapted from Scholastic News *April 2001, Edition 2, Scholastic, Inc., 2001*

Summarizing

With *The Mitten* by Jan Brett

Presented by Kerri Moser and her first-grade class

ummarizing a story requires that students select key information that is important to understanding the story, ignore minor and peripheral details, and put the condensed information into their own words. This process helps them both recognize main ideas and remember what they read. Graphic organizers that feature story sequence, story elements, and the 5 W's are useful for helping students boil down a story to an essential few sentences.

The Mitten is a favorite of reading specialist Kerri Moser. In this Ukrainian folktale, a boy named Nicki loses his white mitten in the snow. One by one, woodland creatures get cozy in the warm mitten until . . . bear gives a great big sneeze. The mitten is forced into the air, where it is spotted by its relieved owner. This linear story is ideal for a lesson on summarizing. Kerri uses a sequencing graphic organizer with her students as an important step to creating a book summary.

LESSON

Preparation

Begin with a discussion about what a summary is and why knowing how to summarize is useful: A summary of a story helps us remember the story; A summary is part of a book review; When a friend asks us about a book we just read or when we want to recommend a book to a friend, we can give them a summary of the book.

Familiarize the children with the sequencing graphic organizer on page 93. Explain that the chart will help us organize information from the story so that they can write a summary. Only the most important information makes it into a summary.

Conduct a picture-walk through the book. Discuss the illustrations and draw attention to important elements such as the setting, the main characters, and so on.

❑ Read the story aloud for enjoyment.

❑ Before rereading, set the purpose for reading: *to listen to the story and gather important information that can be used to summarize the story when it is over.*

❑ Refer to the graphic organizer as you talk about the important events of the story. What should be written in the "First," "Next," "Then," and "Finally" boxes? There may be disagreement about how to fill in the chart. This is a great opportunity to discuss the fact that there is more than one right way to fill it out. While the order of the story's events should always be the same, the detail may vary. And sometimes information is combined.

❏ Read the story one more time, stopping at predetermined points that coincide with the graphic organizer. This will make completing the graphic organizer much easier. I choose to stop at the end of pages 4, 5, 23, and 27. (My page 1 begins on the first page of text.) Our graphic organizer looks like this:

What Happens in *The Mitten*?	
First	Nicki's grandmother knits him a pair of white mittens.
Next	Nicki goes for a walk and loses a mitten in the snow.
Then	One by one, the woodland animals crawl into the mitten to stay warm.
Finally	The bear sneezes and the mitten flies into the air. Nicki finds his mitten and returns home.

❏ As you fill in the graphic organizer, remind students that a summary is short. To keep a summary short a lot of the information is not included. Demonstrate this point by asking students if they should include the way each animal made its way to the mitten. Does there appear to be room on the chart for all that information? Guide them to the conclusion that one sentence can be used to describe everything that happens between page 6 (when the mole discovers the mitten) and page 23 (when the bear sneezes and forces the mitten into the air)—"One by one, the woodland animals crawled into the mitten to stay warm."

❏ Now use the sentences in the chart to write a summary. In this shared writing activity, model how to use transition words such as *first, next, then*, and *finally*. Explain that the purpose of using these transition words is to help organize the sequence, or the order of the important events in the story. Here is a sample summary:

Nicki's grandmother knits him a pair of white mittens. Next, Nicki goes for a walk and loses a mitten in the snow. Then, the woodland animals crawl into the mitten to stay warm. When the bear sneezes, the mitten shoots into the air. Finally, Nicki finds the mitten and returns home.

❏ Explain how summaries are written in our own words, not the author's. Drive this point home by comparing the sentences in your summary with the text.

Lesson Modifications

Provide extra support: Teach a mini-lesson in which students compare details that are important for understanding *The Mitten* with details that are there to make a story more interesting. For example, compare the sentences "And it wasn't long until one of his new mittens dropped in the snow and was left behind" and "When he [the owl] decided to move in also, the mole, the rabbit, and the hedgehog grumbled."

Provide a challenge: Invite students to write a summary based on a new ending to *The Mitten*, such as that Nicki doesn't find his mitten and has to tell Baba that he misplaced it.

Summarizing Activities

1. **Is It Important?** After reading aloud a picture book, create a reproducible with details from the book, or write the details on sentence strips. Have students categorize details that are important to understanding the story or are interesting, but that are not necessary to understanding the story.

2. **Say It in Your Own Words.** Read aloud short passages from picture books and have students practice saying what happened in their own words. Have a few volunteers retell the passage to illustrate the many ways to say the same thing.

3. **Stringing Together a Summary.** Create a reproducible containing eight to ten cut-out sentences based on a recently read story. Some sentences are important details that, when correctly strung together, create a summary of the story. Other sentences are unimportant details from the book that students need to disregard. Tell students how many sentences they can use to create their summary.

More Books for Teaching Summarizing

The following books have simple story lines and a manageable amount of text for lessons on summarizing.

Bear Shadow by Frank Asch (Prentice-Hall, 1985). Bear will do anything to get rid of his pesky shadow.

The Story of Ferdinand by Munro Leaf (Grosset & Dunlap, 2000). This classic about a pacifist bull who is picked for the bullfights in Madrid is a fabulous story about peace and contentment.

The Spider Weaver: A Legend of Kente Cloth by Margaret Musgrove (Blue Sky Press, 2001). This is a beautifully told story of a spider who inspires two local weavers to create an exquisite and unique fabric.

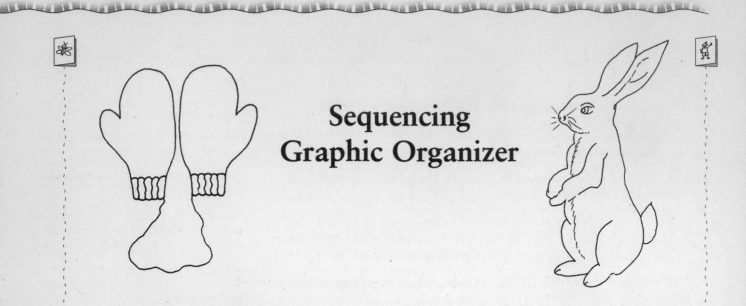

Sequencing
Graphic Organizer

What Happens in *The Mitten*?
First
Next
Then
Finally

Teaching the Essentials of Reading With Picture Books Scholastic Teaching Resources

BIBLIOGRAPHY

Professional Resources

Adams, Marilyn Jager. *Beginning to Read: Thinking and Learning about Print* (Cambridge, MA: MIT Press, paperback edition, February 1994).

Allington, R.L. "Fluency: The Neglected Reading Goal," in *The Reading Teacher* (36, 1983), 556-561.

Armbruster, Bonnie B., Fran Lehr, and Jean Osborn, Center for the Improvement of Early Reading Achievement. *Put Reading First: The Research Building Blocks for Teaching Children to Read,* ed. C. Ralph Adler (Office of Educational Research and Improvement [OERI], U.S. Department of Education, 2001).

Blevins, Wiley. *Phonics from A to Z: A Practical Guide.* (New York: Scholastic, 1998).

Calkins, Lucy McCormick. *The Art of Teaching Reading* (New York: Longman, 2001).

Cunningham, Patricia M., and D. P. Hall, *Making Words: Multilevel, Hands-on, Developmentally Appropriate Spelling and Phonics Activities* (Parsippany, NJ: Good Apple, 1994).

Fox, Barbara J. *Word Identification Strategies,* 2nd ed. (Upper Saddle River, NJ: Merrill, 2000).

Nagy, W.E., and P.A. Herman. "Breadth and Depth of Vocabulary Knowledge: Implications for acquisition and instruction," in *The Nature of Vocabulary Acquisition,* ed. Margaret G. McKeown and Mary E. Curtis (Hillsdale, NJ: Erlbaum Associates, 1987), 19–35.

Nathan, R.G., and K.E. Stanovich. "The Causes and Consequences of Differences in Reading Fluency," in *Theory into Practice* (30, 1991), 176–184.

National Academy of Education. *Becoming a Nation of Readers, the Report of the Commission on Reading,* prepared by Richard C. Anderson (Pittsburgh, National Academy of Education, 1985).

Opitz, Michael F. *Rhymes & Reasons: Literature and Language Play for Phonological Awareness* (Portsmouth, NH: Heinemann, 2000).

Opitz, Michael F., and T.V. Rasinski. *Good-bye Round Robin: 25 Effective Oral Reading Strategies,* ed. Lois Bridges (Portsmouth, NH: Heinemann, 1998).

Rasinski, Timothy V. *The Fluent Reader: Oral Reading Strategies for Building Word Recognition, Fluency, and Comprehension* (New York: Scholastic, 2003).

Rasinski, Timothy V., and N.D. Padak. *From Phonics to Fluency: Effective Teaching of Decoding and Reading Fluency in the Elementary School* (New York: Longman, 2001).

Samuels, S.J., N. Shermer, and D. Reinking. "Reading Fluency: Techniques for Making Decoding Automatic," in *What Research Has to Say About Reading Instruction,* ed. Alan E. Farstrup and S. Jay Samuels, (Newark, DE: International Reading Association, 1992), 124–44.

Picture Books Featured in Lessons

Brett, Jan. *The Mitten* (New York: G.P. Putnam's Sons, 1989).

Buckley, Richard. *The Foolish Tortoise,* illustrated by Eric Carle (Saxonville, MA: Picture Book Studio, 1985).

Cannon, Janell. *Stellaluna* (San Diego: Harcourt Brace Jovanovich 1993).

Carle, Eric. *A House for Hermit Crab* (Saxonville, MA: Picture Book Studio, 1987).

Degen, Bruce. *Jamberry* (New York: Harper & Row, 1983).

Edwards, Pamela Duncan. *Some Smug Slug,* illustrated by Henry Cole (New York: HarperCollins Publishers, 1996).

Ehlert, Lois. *Nuts to You!* (San Diego: Harcourt Brace Jovanovich, 1993).

Havill, Juanita. *Jamaica's Find,* illustrated by Anne Sibley O'Brien (Boston: Houghton Mifflin Co., 1986).

Hutchins, Pat. *The Wind Blew* (New York: Macmillan, 1974).

Lester, Mike. *A Is for Salad* (New York: Putnam & Grosset, 2000).

Munsch, Robert. *Andrew's Loose Tooth,* illustrated by Michael Martchenko (New York: Scholastic Inc., 1998).

Selsam, Millicent, E. *How Puppies Grow,* photos by Esther Bubley (New York: Four Winds Press, 1971).

Shaw, Nancy. *Sheep on a Ship,* illustrated by Margot Apple (Boston: Houghton Mifflin, 1989).

Wood, Don, and Audrey Wood. *The Little Mouse, the Red Ripe Strawberry, and the Big Hungry Bear* (New York: Scholastic, Inc. 1984).

Additional Picture Books and Resources

Appelbaum, Marci, and Jeff Catanese. *Folk Tale Plays From Around the World That Kids Will Love!* (New York: Scholastic, 2002).

Barchers, Suzanne I. *Readers Theatre for Beginning Readers (Grades 1-4),* (New York: Teacher Ideas Press, 1993).

Bemelmans, Ludwig. *Madeline* (New York: Puffin Books, 1998).

Branley, Franklyn M. *Mission to Mars,* illustrated by True Kelley (New York: HarperCollins Publishers, Inc., 2002).

Bridwell, Norman. *Clifford the Big Red Dog* (New York: Scholastic, 1985).

Bynum, Janie. *Altoona Baboona* (San Diego, CA: Harcourt Brace, 1999).

Calmenson, Stephanie. *It Begins with an A,* illustrated by Marisabina Russo (New York: Hyperion Books for Children, 1993).

Carle, Eric. *The Very Clumsy Click Beetle* (New York: Philomel Books, 1999).

———. *The Grouchy Ladybug* (New York: HarperCollins Publishers, 1996).

Cowcher, Helen. *Antarctica* (New York: Farrar, Straus and Giroux, 1990; Big Book edition: New York, Scholastic, 1990).

Crawford, Sheryl Ann, and Nancy I. Sanders. *15 Easy-to-Read Mini Plays (K-2)* (New York: Scholastic, 2002).

Enderle, Judith Ross, and Stephanie Gordon Tessler. *Six Snowy Sheep*, illustrated by John O'Brien (New York: Puffin Books, 1995).

Fleming, Denise. *In the Small, Small Pond* (New York: H. Holt, 1993).

Fox, Mem. *Wilfrid Gordon McDonald Partridge*, illustrated by Julie Vivas (Brooklyn, NY: Kane/Miller Book Publishers, 1985).

Geisel, Theodor Seuss [Dr. Seuss]. *Green Eggs and Ham* (New York: Random House, 1960).

Harjo, Joy. *The Good Luck Cat*, illustrated by Paul Lee (San Diego: Harcourt Brace, 2000)

Henkes, Kevin. *Sheila Rae, the Brave* (New York: Greenwillow Books, 1987).

Holabird, Katherine. *Angelina on Stage*, illustrations by Helen Craig (Middleton, WI: Pleasant Company Publications, 2001).

Hopkins, Lee Bennett. *Alphathoughts: Alphabet Poems*, illustrated by Marla Baggetta (Honesdale, PA: Wordsong/ Boyds Mills Press, 2003).

Kellogg, Steven. *Aster Aardvark's Alphabet Adventure* (New York: William Morrow, 1987).

———. *The Three Little Pigs* (New York: HarperCollins Publishers, 1997).

Leaf, Munro. *The Story of Ferdinand*, illustrated by Robert Dawson (New York: Grosset & Dunlap Publishers, 2000).

Lear, Edward. *An Edward Lear Alphabet*, illustrated by Carol Newsom (New York: Lothrop, Lee & Shepard Books, 1983).

Lewison, Wendy Cheyette. *Clifford's Loose Tooth* (New York: Scholastic, 2002).

Lionni, Leo. *A Color of His Own*. (Albany, NY: Delmar Publishers, 1990)

———. *An Extraordinary Egg* (Big Book edition: New York: Scholastic, 1994).

Livingston, Myra Cohn. *Up in the Air*, illustrated by Leonard Everett Fisher (New York: Holiday House, 1989).

Martinez, Alejandro Cruz. *The Woman Who Outshone the Sun* (Children's Book Press, 1991; Big Book edition: New York, Scholastic, 1991).

McCall, Francis, and Patricia Keeler. *A Huge Hog is a Big Pig: A Rhyming Word Game* (New York: Greenwillow Books, 2002).

McNaughton, Colin. *Suddenly!* (San Diego: Harcourt Brace, 1995).

Modesitt, Jeanne. *Sometimes I Feel Like a Mouse: A Book About Feelings*, illustrated by Robin Spowart (New York: Scholastic, 1992).

Most, Bernard. *A Pair of Protoceratops* (San Diego: Harcourt Brace, 1998).

———. *A Trio of Triceratops* (San Diego: Harcourt Brace, 1998).

Munsch, Robert. *Alligator Baby*, illustrated by Michael Martchenko (New York: Scholastic, Inc., 2002).

Musgrove, Margaret. *The Spider Weaver: A Legend of Kente Cloth*, illustrated by Julia Cairns (New York: Blue Sky Press, 2001).

Numeroff, Laura. *If You Take a Mouse to School*, illustrated by Felicia Bond (New York: Laura Geringer Books, HarperCollins Publishers, 2002).

Phillips, Joan. *Lucky Bear*, illustrated by J. P. Miller (New York: Random House, 1986).

Rockwell, Anne. *Becoming Butterflies*, pictures by Megan Halsey (New York: Walker & Company, 2002).

Ryder, Joanne. *Big Bear Ball*, illustrations by Steven Kellogg (New York: HarperCollins Publishers, 2002).

Schaefer, Lola M. *What's Up, What's Down?* pictures by Barbara Bash (New York: Greenwillow Books, 2002).

Schwartz, Alvin. *Busy Buzzing Bumblebees and Other Tongue Twisters*, illustrated by Paul Meisel (New York: HarperCollins Publishers, 1992).

Shaw, Nancy. *Raccoon Tune*, illustrated by Howard Fine (New York: Henry Holt and Company, 2003).

Steig, William. *Doctor De Soto* (New York: Farrar, Straus and Giroux, 1997).

Waddell, Martin. *Owl Babies*, illustrated by Patrick Benson (Cambridge, MA: Candlewick Press, 1992).

Weeks, Sarah. *Mrs. McNosh Hangs up Her Wash*, pictures by Nadine Bernard Westcott (New York: Laura Geringer Books, 1988).

Williams, Vera B. *A Chair for My Mother* (New York: Greenwillow Books, 1982; Big Book edition: New York, Scholastic, 1992).

Yolen, Jane. *How Do Dinosaurs Get Well Soon?* illustrated by Mark Teague (New York: Blue Sky Press, 2003).

Books in the Following Easy-Reader Series

Curious George books by H.A. Rey and Margret Rey

Frog and Toad books by Arnold Lobel

George and Martha books by James Marshall

Henry and Mudge books by Cynthia Rylant

Little Bear books by Else Minarik